THE COLORS OF LIFE

The International Library of Poetry

Howard Ely, Editor

The Colors of Life

Library of Congress
Cataloging in Publication Data

ISBN 0-7951-5239-6

Proudly manufactured in the United States of America by
Watermark Press
One Poetry Plaza
Owings Mills, MD 21117

The International Library of Poetry
poetry.COM

FOREWORD

Throughout life, we store information collected from experiences and try in some way to make sense of it. When we are not able to fully understand the things that occur in our lives, we often externalize the information. By doing this, we are afforded a different perspective, thus allowing us to think more clearly about difficult or perplexing events and emotions. Art is one of the ways in which people choose to externalize their thoughts.

Within the arts, modes of expression differ, but poetry is a very powerful tool by which people can share sometimes confusing, sometimes perfectly clear concepts and feelings with others. Intentions can run the gamut as well: The artists may simply want to share something that has touched their lives in some way, or they may want to get help to allay anxiety or uncertainty. The poetry within *The Colors of Life* is from every point on the spectrum: every topic, every intention, every event or emotion imaginable. Some poems will speak to certain readers more than others, but it is always important to keep in mind that each verse is the voice of a poet, of a mind that needs to make sense of this world, of a heart that feels the effects of every moment in this life, and perhaps of a memory that is striving to surface. Nonetheless, recalling our yesterdays gives birth to our many forms of expression.

Cover art: "Oak Leaves" by Domonique Dials

No One

No one can see
No one can hear
All things inside
That cause my fear
Nothings working
Nothings right
My thoughts are as clear
As the dead of night
Something scary
Something wrong
Something that caused
My awful song
Thing that's horrid
Thing that's bad
I feel like
I've been had
No one can see
No one can hear
All things inside
That cause my fear

Emma Louise Johnson

Dear Daddy

I miss the dinners out with the lobster tails,
the movies and the books,
and the crazy man swimming in the pool
during lightning storms.
I miss hearing your voice on the phone.
I miss the Sunday drives of long ago,
and the potato pancakes.
Oh, and how I miss the "Heavens to Betsy,"
the chocolate and nuts,
the stupid jokes,
and even "In-A-Gadda-Da-Vida."
When I dream of you you're young and strong,
your hands were warm and
full of strength.
That is how I will think of you
and remember you,
with your gimlets, your laughter, your voice
saying, "I love you, Lulu."

Leah McNamara

My River

My river is a thief,
Stealing my heart
And running away
With the sun's gold,
The moon's silver,
Bits of brown
And pieces of green
From the forest floor.
Throwing crystals in the air
As it dashes over jagged rocks,
Merry-go-rounding in eddies,
Diving in wild abandonment
Over the falls,
Until, with foam-crowned head,
It brings its bounty
To life's first home.

William Patrick Benoit

I Found the Garden of Eden in Manhattan

Crossing the invisible threshold of the park,
I was enveloped in a quilt of trees.
The hands of the breeze massaged my back
as my worries seemed to fall asleep
on the feathery pillows of clouds above.
Boisterous voices of discontent
faded from my soul's ears.
Inundated in a baptism of quietness,
no longer able to run, stillness caught me.
Just as from a dream, I awoke,
dancing in the grandeur of God's creation.
I was surrounded, everywhere a multitude,
each begun with a divine spark:
See the children! Feel the warmth of the sun!
Each pounded awe and humility on me,
steadfastly demanding, "Acknowledge your Creator!"
As if seeing you, I let go of my bike,
I spread my arms outwards.
Free, I soar as with eagle's wings.

Brian Henri Kranick

Admonition to the Fog

You painted out our mountains
and our trees
the way ceramic students
brush two coats of milky glaze
upon a lovely figurine.
You narrowed down our world
like Poe's dread pendulum
closed in the pit.
And though we know
the glaze will bake away
when nature's kiln
transcends the eerie sky,
we find it difficult
this seventh day
to smile,
when claustrophobia
sits down with us again
at suppertime.

Katherine Higgins

Winter Tree Finger Painting

In freelance fashion, winter tree,
you cast your offering to the sunrise.
No adornment, self-sustained beauty,
you etch your silhouette against the skies.
Throughout the day . . . hospitality,
host . . . congenial bird bearer.
Excluding no nationality.
Vagrant snowflake, rainy wayfarer,
our evening tree-clasp is of gentle yield
to the evening sunset amber light.
Finger painting poignant shadows upon lake and field.
You bough and bid your sweet good night.

Winifred L. Gonyea

Priority As the Obsidian of Truth

Telling the fortune in a bowl of fish,
watching cold, stumbling, golden animals
reticulated by the fate of watching eyes,
objectively, the woman applied contentment.
Her formulation was programmed by
the tiny mice in an incandescent
arc rising from the presence of the sun,
setting in the craters of the moon,
magnetic, idealistic, empty, and awaiting
a collection of variables.
Dependence creasing defiance, challenges,
insight warbled essentials as they passed between
surfaces and congealed along the edges.
Doubled, tripled, the slightest image
of obscure sensitivity, the right hand,
the black glass reflected, manipulated,
the resource sculpting inevitability to
make a tract, awkward icons swimming.

Baron Joseph A. Uphoff, Jr.

Artist's Profile

Eli Kavon

Sunrise, Florida, USA

Despite persecution and discrimination, the Jewish people have survived and thrived. I am the link in the chain of a 3000-year-old tradition. I am proud to bear that responsibility. The poem "The Son of Prophets" expresses this pride.

The Son of Prophets

I am the son of prophets,
Of nomads, mad, damned, unknown,
I am the scion of refugees
Of those who wandered the world
Never knowing rest or respite.

I am the architect of destiny
The inheritor of an ancient foundation stone
And the blueprint of a glorious heritage
Passed down from parent to child.

God throbs in a nation's soul
In a people that mastered memory
Singed by the fires of hate
Burned in the arsons of history.

I am the son of skeletons
Brought to life
Flesh covers their bones
They are alive
Their message will never die.

Eli I. Kavon

Etude on Memory

It was heard as a distant chime
Whispering faintly in fatigue
Even as evening clouds climb
Over molding hills in critique
I wasn't there on foreign land
Mesmerized with intrigue
Should memory willingly expand
Embracing a questioned technique
How could such event even arise
From undisturbed times askew
My soul must, in senility, demise
Returning to a world I once knew
Oh clear the tune; now is sublime!
Strain not memory's effort in prime
Litienmin

Richard J. Lee

Timetable

In due time, a span of time, in the
course of a lifetime, inside a millennium.
When meantime while just standing there dilly-
dallying, passing time, wasting time, and
killing time, but only for the time being.
Yet at the whole time, creeping,
crawling, and sliding, never at any time
stopping to ask for time. However, at some
time or other, in complete disregard of time
altogether.
I stop at hang time simply because it
requires too much time to talk about time
at any given time.

Gil Prado

Artist's Profile

Gloria Rapp

Tucson, Arizona, USA

For me, poetry reveals itself through inspirational moments . . . like shelling beans with my mother. Those magic moments in life allow me to find unusual forms of expression in poetry or praise. I'm grateful that, for me, my soul reveals itself through poetic form. It cleanses my soul and keeps memories clear. I am now making my own cards, and my poetry finds its way into each occasion. I am presently compiling my poetry into a book for publication. I'm actively working on my dream.

So Many "Lasts"

Mom and I shelled the last of the beans Dad planted before his death,
a truly awesome experience knowing that phase of our life was over.
Last weekend my sister weeded the remains of the garden.
She harvested the last Vidalia onions from last fall's planting . . .
That last harvest was gigantic!
From that time he spent with hoe in hand
and oftentimes on his knees . . . onwards 'til his death,
We marveled at the energy Dad
mustered just to plant his garden.
None of us know what was in his heart,
or on his mind. . . .
We just know we benefited from the love he put into the soil.
He must have known his time was near
for he poured all his sweetness into those beans and onions.
None have ever come close to the
texture and the taste of this love . . .
so tenderly nurtured by his hands,
in the composted soil he diligently
harvested, never wasting anything,
finding use in everything . . . for our benefit.

Gloria Gastellum Rapp

Andree

Somewhere in Luxembourg,
15 years old,
your thighs just blossoming
into womanhood,
you were one of the lucky Jews
hastened out of Europe
before the Blitz Krieg,
before the death camps
tortured and gassed
your siblings and cousins,
just a child—
you were brought to America
to bear their pain forever.

Frank J. Antonazzi, Jr.

multiracial in a small town

don't laugh at my plaid skin
while yours, white wonder
is so pure and clean
and your scorn is like knives
in my multicolored back
see the blood? it's red, like yours
but peroxide will never befriend me
and i don't care about khaki clothes
you won't get me
white wonder bread people
you can't catch me
i'll never be blue and blonde and white all over
so laugh and point and shout
but you can never change me
while your shutters close on me
and your sprinklers rain on me
and your dog, it growls
and your mama calls the police
when all i want you to do
is come out and play

Bethann Cleary

Artist's Profile

Edi Johnson

Tucson, Arizona, USA

The operational intelligence of this world that scientists, doctors, and philosophers only discover a little about and give all sorts of names: nature, biology, all ologies, really is actually Cosmic Mind that is "Extra-Terrestrial." We neither possess or control it. Poetry puts me in touch with that mind with God, I believe. Thanks for publishing "Spring Dying."

Spring Dying

My mother died on seventeenth April,
and ever since that springtime loss
out of strained rainbow coats of piety,
there's this silver leaf I keep trying to glimpse.
It's back of a dark cloud flying up out of night
like the idea of sunrise must surely have flown
to shatter God's gloom and make him think, "Children!"

To know divine Love, it must be sought, must come to rest
along the cave mysteries of hearts,
which are clouds' realities; vague kindness of sight
that shields us from startling days
of watching earth loves arrive, then go.

And this silver leaf trembles awhile, then flies
up from stains on every church glass
framing wind and marrow of spirit in us,
some hope that blossoming will grow out of rain
of Aprils when all those light, green things
seem touched by death, somehow, for me
since she left me bereft at that deadly spring.

Edi Johnson

Artist's Profile

Scott Ishman

Aloha, Oregon, USA

I was living in Ireland with my family in a small village named Maynouth. In the morning I used to walk to work along the bank of a canal. This morning stood out for some reason.

Today I Walked at Eye Level with Water

Today I walked at eye level with water,
Through walls of earth taking itself back.
I saw circles make themselves over again,
From nothing.
I walked through a ring of halves.
One older than my homeland,
The other as new as the day.
I took in the essence of a foreign plant,
And felt my being seep into the surround.

Scott Edward Ishman

Regret

Ill-repaired and tether cut,
I drifted with the wind.
Blue eyes the sea that took me there.

Hello so soon, I fell for her
Like a busted satellite.

And that month became like rain on the Sahara.

Forgotten all that first was told,
Wrought out in seasons past.
Affection's clock ticked its last;
Rewound, it started over.

Stories of old, stories of love
Wheeling me in on a gurney.
My wings she gently mended.

And summer's beard was gray and long.

Wealth did lose its value.
The street still warm beneath me,
I stood there in the dark,
A king without a castle; a cloud without a sky.

Goodbye the coldest word of all;
My one regret: goodbye.

Eric John Peltz

Yesterday

To Jimmy with love and thanks
The computer crashed.
The cat got sick.
I spent all my money on coffee and cigarettes.
But that was yesterday.
Today you said you loved me.
Drank coffee like a drunk drinks wine
Till my body trembled like a leaf in the wind
Then I couldn't sleep and cried all night.
But that was yesterday.
Today you said you loved me.
I try to remember all the things you said
Tomorrow isn't here--yesterday's dead.
And right this moment you love me.
Let me lie in your arms
And take away the pain of all my yesterdays
And promise this moment you will help me
Get over yesterdays
And overcome my fear of tomorrows
Because you love me.
Do you still?

Janet Marie Easton

Buckets and Tobacco

The bleached skeleton
of a '71 Buick in a front yard with ATVs
cruising Main Street.
One-horse towns are erased quietly from maps
and famous names rubbed from collective memories.

Dogs treat you as a friend—
friendlier than people.
There is no expectation that beliefs are the same.
Small steps progressing through
drops of pine trees and maple crackles.
A natural rhythm by which life is carried
in syrup buckets or tobacco fields.

Buckets sometimes are traded for
guns—a limb here—
extension of the body.
Of the women, I can only say
they are braver in this April.

Dave Jones

The Unicorn's Festival of Joy

Harps of moonlight ivory,
Play for unicorns tonight,
Lovely melodies and notes,
Dance with the joyous light.

Music of sunlight gold,
Twirl around laughing dancers,
Songs circle 'round the hooves,
Especially for the prancers.

Wings of starlight feathers,
Lift gleeful dancers in the air,
Stardust spirals down to the floor,
As a stallion sings with his mare.

Voices of cloud-light pearls,
Sing to the heavenly sky,
High and low, blend together
As happy friendship tightly tie.

Harmony of unicorn diamonds,
Brings old enemies together,
Smiles and Laughter have come tonight,
And all hearts lift like feathers.

Stephanie Yoon Ji Song

his tower

he rested the next block on top
with concentrated fingers like a singer
mouth hung open—hoping that the shrill
in his next note would quote
muted memories to all those who listened
he eyed the append to his tower and cowered
at every tremble, every shake, quake
and promise to topple and fall
as he scolded us for breathing too hard
while mind labeling the remaining pieces
on the table starting from first here to last
as he ascended past—past columns
with "next" in his hand but too fast
that the airs quivered the wrath of movement
lost its regal balance to heaven and returned
to choke on a ground that devoured its
luminance—so he bent his head back and
grappled his hair that twisted underneath his
palms—looked at the empathy on our faces
and laughed because it wasn't that serious

Lorra J. Jackson

Coffee Shop Faint

"You're a special kind of girl,"
he said without conviction.
His voice came to me distant, stilted, strangled.
I looked at his disconnected smile.
I didn't want to hear him lie to me,
but he wouldn't stop.
"I think I'm in love with you," he continued
and his eyes glazed over like a doughnut.
I wanted to scream.
I tried to punch him as hard as I could,
right on his fatuous, beakish nose,
but it ended up a flirtatious feint.
He caught my fist, pried it flat, held my now-limp hand,
"Are you listening to me? I said, 'I think I love you.'"
He repeated pointlessly, twice, "I love you."
(His voice was as hollow as the words it carried.)
I started to fade, then: The airless coffee shop disintegrated,
what could I do but float away?
It was his fault, anyway, he started it:
you should mean it if you say a thing like that.

Rebekah Rachel McCoy

Artist's Profile

Mary Lloyd

Marietta, Georgia, USA

Poetry has always been a way for me to express my thoughts, and it flows quite easily for me. I was working in a bindery at a print shop and listening to my coworkers gossip about other coworkers. Christians say, "There but for the grace of God, I." The Buddhist might say, "There through the grace of creation go I."

Buddhist in a Bindery

As day of drudge, judgements fly
As mouths blast out opinions, negative, misplaced go by

Unknowing facts shared by ears, attached to curious critical minds
Mindless beyond the imagined points, judgements issued freely all kinds

Liberal shapes, details eschewed foibles of un-intent
Disaster soon created where doldrums may present

Words, whispers, innuendoes, who did what, when
Who was where, how, who knows, how again

Fantasy issued in negativity's bards, violence hints to be
Expression of euphemisms explode into someone's reality

Truth, unnecessary bind, uninteresting crime
Who needs it? Critics' corner has no time

Dull, witless, innocent delight comes with tales of woe
Molded in unknown facts, spun like nets to catch the foe

A victim hit, the bard finding its touch
The center mark, too much

Free me of this bombarding foil, move my ears beyond the sound
Find a space of peace and tranquility, clear my being of influences
That abound, yes, then this world will speak of me, a critical mess
Filled with villainous facts, no less; filled in mindful emptiness

Mary Lloyd

The Pre-Ascension

In sterile cold you glisten,
Your perfect emptiness
Rigid on stainless steel.
Behind your head of matted hair,
I pool with you
Into puddles of stagnant memories.
Beautiful one
In pieces now . . .
The isolation of my completeness
Overwhelms me.
I slip with you,
Into a bag, wet and sticky
Zipped up and discarded.

Keith R. Ostrowski

Mis-Praise

He beat the keys,
disfiguring the music.
Concentrating on perfecting
our torture,
he strained, as his fingers
tripped and stumbled over
their victims.

When he finished,
he breathed in a great breath,
reveling in his massacre.

And they applauded louder
than if Beethoven had been their executioner.

Adassa Mae Richardson

Artist's Profile

Maria Rivas

Buenos Aires, Argentina

I am a chair professor at the University of the Merchant Marine and director of the language department of the same university. My poem appeals to the old Stone-Age figurines found in caves in France rather than the Greek goddess of love. It conveys the echoes of an early time when man was closer to the divinity, to the Mother Earth, the great provider of life, able to give rebirth at any time.

Venus

My red clay womanhood. Could be.
Pieces of me sliding deep down this spiral carnelian groove.
And I bring forth of myself. Without consort. Still a maiden.
My whole self being stitched up
hatched over and over again.
Most perplexing! At least it seems so.
How my ballooning breasts thread down
and fumble the abyss of my groin.
How my hips track down in crescents
to prowl my inadequate feet.
How the moonbeams seep through my blood

nest my womb lullabying my bubble eggs.

I'm gownless
unaware of the secrecy of my filiations
totally uncharted
weaving the meshes of my otherness.

Maria V. Rivas

Prayer 37

Red sportscar.
Handsome hunk.
Prayer 37.
Why does God grant me
good handwriting,
flaky crust,
and close parking spaces
but not prayer 37.

Kim D. Sievers

Rita's Tears

Setting sun glowing through dirty windows
turning hospital bedding yellow, matching
jaundiced skin as Rita ended with pearly
tear drops forming in the corner of one
closed eye, swelling, then gliding down
smoothly to chapped mouth which would no
more say, "I'm gonna beat this, Charles,
I'm gonna beat it," yeah

Long day ending since the call asking me
to be holding her small hand, hearing
anguished screaming, still echoing today,
then precious last minutes, she breathing
slower, slower, and I kissed the last
tear when Rita was no more

Charles Larsen

In Silence She Moves

I write to you before any sun protrudes
From nights velvet shroud
Before pixie dust has been removed from
your eyes. And as I watch you lie in bed,
a soft smile about your lips
I move across your thoughts, unknown to you, yet familiar.
Unrevealed in presence, I press upon you
in spirit, silently I trace the echoes of your heart's beat.
A slow steady song it plays for those willing to listen.
O, upon the nights wind your hearts
lyrics ride,
Its words soft and sweet.
In distance its sound fades with
morning's light, so sleep gentle lover,
an angel watches over you in mid heaven.

J. Scott Trimble

sand in your shoe

one finger
standing tall
in defiance
of everything you stand for
all you abused sulking in dimly lit coffee shops
wrapped up in spite and self-pity
because no one understands how deep you are
we all feel pain
we all die a million tiny deaths
at the hands of others
we have all been at the mercy of fate
like ants under a magnifying glass
like a deer in the headlights
drink down fire
burn down trees
gargle with every ounce of your impotent rage
then quit complaining
you have the power to weave words into magic
if you could just get over yourself for a second

Sean S. McMahon

Artist's Profile

Michael Dodson

Milan, Texas, USA

Inspiration comes from the strangest of places. There is, of course, nothing special about toast, or is there? You never know what has touched the life of something or someone. A forgotten stub of pencil, a coin on the sidewalk; everything has a story. A poem, even: On a certain Thursday, I, unsatisfied with life and uncertain of the future, wrote 116 small poems, with all the finesse of the stereotypical dark and moody teenager. Yet even the roughest ore produces fine gems, as number seventy-six of 116 indeed proved to be.

oddpoem076

there is such magnitude
in a piece of toast

the bread was made with flour and water
and baked in an oven lovingly built
by a factory worker in Iowa
with a wife and two children
and a pet dog named Goldy
and the water was purified with chlorine tablets
made by a struggling artist in a lab in Peru
while the flour came from the Gale farm
and the wheat ripened in the golden sun
watched by a girl who dreamed about rainbows
and emerald cities

and when someone asks you what
you ate for lunch
you can say
a small piece
of Kansas

Michael L. Dodson

Artist's Profile

Tanarra Schneider

Chicago, Illinois, USA

Tanarra Meryan hails from Chicago where she dances, and works, and writes, and creates, and loves. The story behind the poem is not as important as the feeling, and the feeling is that need, that desire to express to someone a particular someone, and be denied, be completely denied. The most essential thing I do as a writer is listen. And as a friend, I listen. And I try to translate what I hear into words. And whatever comes out is my poetry.

Talkin' Up the Talk

blah, blah, blah . . .
8 days, 8 days, 8 days
2 rings, 2 hours, 2 words
hey, stranger

performed your usual rhetoric
Me me me Me
questions, why's, how's, concern and communication left to
anyone else and beneath you
Somehow
Blah Blah Blah
Ma Bell laughed at me as I listened to your me-isms
not out of interest—but due to intense gluttony and
apparent lack of self control

Blah, Me, Blah, Mine, Blah . . .
After exhausting the tales of you and you and your's thoughts
you politely skipped to good night
Sending me to bed
with a mouth full of words to pick out of my teeth in the morning
Blah!

Tanarra Schneider

Inside Me

There is a place deep inside me . . .
And as I open the door . . .
There are beaded curtains and as you look out,
There are gypsies singing and dancing,
With their skirts twirling like flowers.
You dance and sing with them 'til dawn.
Then you are the King of Pirates,
Plundering the Seven Seas.
As you go below the deck,
You're mining treasures with dwarfs.
You rescue dukes and dames
Leaning forward on your gallant steed.
Or you are as small as a mouse.
Swim with mermaids, fly with fairies,
Underwater worlds and a giant's house.
Anything can happen here.
Climb my beanstalk,
My world,
My secret place,
Inside me.

Emily Rose Anderson

Citrus Girl

Her tangerine face,
chambered and bruising,
reflects tease-peeled pieces
of puddled flesh,
sectioned,
and dripping with time.

Lauren Elaine McDonald

Changes

I think of the times I sat in my room and cried,
"I can't wait to leave—grow up—move out!"
It all seemed so idealic.
Now it's looming and I want to run, so afraid,
Petrified of life,
Scares me so much I want to hide
Deep under my covers which have always protected
From monsters—the dark—
Myself.
So what do I do now? Where do I go? Who do I see?
I'll miss you all . . .
Yes, you,
Who made me cry, who made me laugh, who made me despise myself
Love myself, be myself
And anyone BUT myself.
This will be my last hurrah,
For what will distinguish me from the billions now?
Nothing except my face, so easily forgotten,
Turned unseen twards these people I hate, whispering,
"I love you."

Dianne Jean Aikey

I Watched My Father Drown

I watched my father drown
not at sea all sound and fury
fighting to stay afloat in
a world of ordinary things
that to him had lost all meaning
struggling for air amongst tides
of partly remembered faces
until exhausted with the effort
he released his grip and
spiraled down.

Stephen Brinksman

primate blurb

atheist dreams, silent screams, abortion in
a muddy stream. cool aqua inhale. coffee
stains resident pains, seek to find spring
in a bottle (still). the primate i hate,
propagate apostasy. neglected and swollen
like sudden swift abandon, calling out from
bleeding pores and what's in store, the masses
implore. contortionist volition, singing
redolent prose. albumen ready for consumption
asinine leisure, legionary lesion and
corrupt masturbation.

David Clark

Old Bill

Three months of drought shattered.
I think we were all in shock. Nobody knew what to do,
just stared forlornly out wet glass, dribbled
out in twos and threes onto the new mud.
Stared up.
All that long collection of dry, dead
dust sucking the sweat from my face and
hair for those months started running down into my mouth,
I almost felt guilty shedding that dust so quick,
after it had been with me so long.
Across the street, then, Old Bill screamed.
I still remember it. Take disbelief, wonder, and
all the joy you could pack into one man's vocal cords.
Now make it real loud.
That's what Old Bill's scream was.
And whatever it was that held us there, that broke it.
People were laughing, crying,
Dancing in circles with their mouths up and open.
Hot damn, that was life falling on them then.
And they knew it.

Ed Goobie

Artist's Profile

Rebecca Paolino

Watertown, Connecticut, USA

I currently am a student a Westover School in Connecticut, and "Simone's Abetone" is my debut in poetry. Simone was my great-grandfather who lived and worked in Tuscany, Italy, on the great Mt. Abetone. The stories of his life on Abetone were often recounted at family gatherings,and I longed to immortalize him in verse. I hope that not only my relatives can appreciate the sacrifices of this man but also the readers of "The Colors of Life."

Simone's Abetone

In Tuscany among olivy vales,
knotted trees scatter hillsides.
Mt. Abetone dwarfs the Apennines's range
and casts looming shadows on surrounding Piedmont cities.

From this raw landscape is molded
my great-grandfather, Simone,
whose visage mirrors the mountain's rugged sides
in a mosaic of years, toil, and hardship.

Simone's life belongs to the provincial village of Pève Pelago
where he carves chalk, limestone, and marble Italian Saints:
Santa Caterina, Lucia, Clara, his divine muses.
Mounting the weaving trails up Abetone by mule, he tires,
jolting along the twisted path to reach his secluded quarry.

The secrets of his craft from ancestral masters are evidenced
by gesso and marble dust in his palms, wrinkles, and cuticles.
On his return from the quarry he is redolent with
faint odors of the old rock and limestone.
Man and mountain emerge as one.

Rebecca Paolino

Another Notch in My Belt

The boy was really no more than a face,
a stray dog I persuaded to follow
me up the ladder to his tip-top bunk.
And after a few days he did just that,
rung after anticipated rung.
We were still lying next to each other
in vain silence from the awkwardness that
spilled itself out over the cloud-soft sheets.
In that grey dawn just below the ceiling
I changed my mind, but he still kissed me.
Struggling to keep control, his hands were
eager and icy as he ignored, no.
In a dizzy flash I hit the ceiling
and fell unconscious into him, as he
softly held my head against his chest.

Carol Smith

Children of God . . .

Stars of wonder, stars of night;
Sparks that fell from Perfect Light
When the universe began.
Embers for the soul of man.
How I wonder . . .
What did You want to be when you grew
Up until the time You knew the truth
That Father worked not only wood
But galaxies and stars
Up above the world so high.
You, Who filled the universe with suns
To set the record of Your days
And keep Infinity to watch and wait;
You have all the time in the world.
Father of Inception, Creator of All
And all unknown, Spirit of Conception,
Grant that I may know what do You make of me,
The child of ancient earth and bone?
In all Eternity, what do You hope
Of me alone?

Patricia A. Patka

Artist's Profile

Erin Studer

Sherman Oaks, California, USA

Many of my poems, including "My Cousin," are based on events in my life. To me poetry, is a way to record a story or moment in my family's history. Through this record, I wish to illuminate my experience as well as honor the strength and perseverance of my family. I believe one of the greatest things poetry and, in fact, all literature can do is to provide deeper understanding of other's lives; I hope "My Cousin" has done that.

My Cousin

My aunt looked like skin without bones
when she got out of the car, home from the hospital.
She had given birth to a 6 lb 3 oz. baby girl
who'd been strangled for forever by the umbilical cord.
Too much irony for my four-year-old mind.

Grandmother was the first to tell me of my lifeless cousin just born.
Her never-to-be brother and I were at the breakfast table.
He began to cry; I stayed still. After all, it was his mother, his sister,
but really he was a month older and understood things more quickly.

That afternoon he and I dug a hole
by the ash tree that held one half of the swing set.
"A grave for my sister," he said.

When his mother came home and was helped from the car he ran to her.
Oh, what a small wind could have picked her up and flown her away

She was so empty.
He grasped to her leg to weigh her down.
I stayed by the tree pushing handfuls of dirt
into a Folger's coffee can:
working away at the hole that was too small
to hold a baby's coffin.

Erin Studer

Tapestry

I do not loom my life alone,
A solitary weaver;
Dawn to dusk the shuttle flies
With color from a flaming cloud
Or silver from a star,
The rich and glowing threads
Of loving friends,
A singing tree,
A soothing wind,
A thousand moods and manners
That create a life design.
I do not weave my
Intricate brocade alone
My hand is held within
A larger hand, that when
I let it, moves in shining ways.
Mysterious, it will create,
In spite of flaws
And labored length,
A tapestry of value.

Marjorie Houghton Bates

Perhaps

Perhaps I am Sisyphus meant to carry my
burdens alone,
To struggle to a level of achievement,
only to find it is all an illusion
to have my load crash all around me,
only to be lifted again.
If this is true, so be it, for I only lose
when I don't enjoy the work.
Perhaps I am the Phoenix meant to have many
lives within,
to have my world go in cycles, to have all
around me grow common,
to self-destruct with the flames of my
excess and desires.
If this is true, so be it, for I only lose
when I fail to rise again.
And perhaps I am Tantalus,
meant to have you put before me
to gaze upon and desire
but to share just a fraction of you
before having you wrenched away when I reach
out to touch.
If this is true, so be it, for I only lose
when I fail to stretch out.

Brian Heavey

Artist's Profile

Jo Newton

Sun City West, Arizona, USA

Occasionally, I allow myself to indulge in an oversized helping of nostalgia. Fall has always been my most favorite time of year, dating back to my childhood memories of three birthdays and an anniversary celebrated along with the magnificent explosion of color all around us. The vision of leaves turning from a healthy green into a brilliant spectacle of loveliness will live with me forever. Never to forget the crackling of sun-dried grass beneath my feet, I applaud nature in all its grandeur. Thus this poem, "Seasoned with Love," evolved—it is short, lest I become maudlin.

Seasoned with Love

When the jams and jellies are jarred,
And the garden has reached its peak,
When the bouquet of chili-sauce floats over the yard,
It's Illinois in September that I seek.

When the honey stands in jars of gold,
And bushels are piled with apples so red,
When at crossroad stands these things are sold,
It's to Illinois in October that I'm led.

When the corn stalks are crumbling brown,
And the pumpkins bright orange glow,
When the smoke of burning leaves hangs over the town,
It's the Illinois in November that I know.

It's all these things that I taste, smell, touch, and see,
Plus the flight of the morning dove,
It's the pets and the people so dear to me,
It's Illinois in the fall that I love.

Jo Newton

Fly

I walk slowly through the garden,
Our garden, our home.
My arms stretch out to drink in the sun.
The cool breeze running through my fingers;
I know, my love, that you are near,
Though I cannot see you or hear you or feel you.
We are always together, and forever apart.
Our passion makes us one,
Our love will last this sweet, sentimental moment.
It will feel like forever.
You, my lord of hawks, so strong and sure, in flight.
I, your temptress, who wishes to fly with you.
Forever in flight, like forever in love,
For to fly is to be free.
To be free is to be wild.
To be wild is to live.
To live is to love.
And to love is for the spirit to fly.
I want to fly.

Adrianne Bolt

Untitled

I dreamt of lilies in a whirlpool of hair,
Like a tattoo gone astray. . . .
I heard the whisper of the blue-green ocean
Holding back the day.
I saw the crashing wave of your furrowed brow
Pounding on white beaches of solitary islands,
Swirling colors of deep blues and white
Like Van Gogh's "Starry Night"
I felt the intense gaze of the tide
Pull and lull me in to look into the reflection
Of a scarred moon-soul
Dancing on the ripples of a blue sky-ocean.
Shyly, I traced the pattern in the hair,
But the little butterfly-angels
Wouldn't play fair.

Jon Mabale

The Quiet Night

All the dawns are fast asleep
The toys are put away
Your teddy bear has closed his eyes
So there goes another day
Gently now it's time to go
Into the quiet night
Your puppy dog has drifted off

Jenna Marie Racine

tide (current of the currency of my heart)

you're human driftwood
and now i stand
two stories below you,
one story to you.

you're human driftwood
reciever in hand
nothing more than a fistful of nickles.

you're human driftwood
place your tongue in my ear
attempt to taste what I hear
wrap your legs around my heart
attempt to warm me primally.

but you're just human driftwood.

just human driftwood.

John Edward Glennon

Artist's Profile

Maria McAllister

Los Angeles, California, USA

Grappling with emotions too intense to act out inspires verse. Anger was the dynamic of those terse personal words that gurgled, then splattered the contents of my heart. Non-expectations were challenged by one who claimed self-sage. My fear finally unlocked and I said yes. One thing I couldn't guess was that his fear still crippled, then tripped over mine. Expressions were necessary—I wanted to lash out! A poem formed; I e-mailed this one. Then I came upon the contest and thought, "Why the hell not? No harm, no foul." And now this love story has begun.

Chastity Revisited

Grappling with emotions terse . . . inspires verse.
Needles and pins pinching my breasts,
tracing lines along them as roadmaps.
Butterflies struggled to get out
from this once naked chest.

Ouch! Push them back into their places . . .
no more graces for what never had to be
promised and declared not to lie.

Don't need a map of the heart, the mind, the
depths of a well that may be more shallow
than full. . . .

Catch the firelight and snuff it dry.
Moonglow is more shy than the sun I bathe
in—
Nothing was ever a necessary cry.

Hence the lull. . . .

Maria McAllister

Drifting

I'm moving on again.

Sagebrush is a homeless thing.
The wind blows her about,
banging her against rocks and fences.
She stops only a moment,
waiting for the wind to catch her breath.
There, where she waits, she starts to build,
digging in roots,
scratching for something to cling onto.
But the wind, renewed, rips her up,
tears out her new roots,
and begins again its endless chase.

I'm moving on again.

Terri Karsten

As Always

She sees me coming from across the hall
A big grin on my face
As always

I see her by her locker
Leaning, tired
As always

I start to tell her all that went on
She listens
Or does she?
She is just quietly leaning
Waiting for me to finish

I want her to be full of stories too
Full of laughter
Full of life
Not a hint of a smile
Not even a flash
As always

Fatema Zohra

Artist's Profile

Tanya L. Doyle

Cincinnati, Ohio, USA

I have been writing poems since I was a child as an outlet to express my emotions and feelings. My husband, Rick, and I were recently married and this poem sprang from the emotions of a new bride. Rick's first book, "Date Smart!" came to him after seventeen years as a relationship therapist, and he urged me to enter this contest. His clinical and practical zeal combined with my emotional and poetic flow should make for a great relationship book in the future. What our parents' personalities contributed to our own defines how we came to find each other.

Hand-Delivered Love

His huge, rough, hands; calloused from years of backbreaking work.
No amount of balm could ever soften them.
These hands brushed dirt from a scraped knee, wiped a tear-stained face.
The hands plaiting a little girl's hair, soft & gentle as a queen's.
Through hard ridges and jagged cuticles, he delivered his love.
Often, hands gently eased new life from a birth canal into this world.
Cracked, bleeding hands left a Christmas fire to tend the livestock.
A worn hand patiently pointed out wonders never seen by young eyes.
His, searching & wise; mine, curious & eager.
How I loved those hands!
Now, as he places mine in another's, these memories
come rushing back.
As my eyes well with tears, I fancy that I see a misting in his.
A smile lights my face as I turn to my new husband.
The circle is complete through Daddy's hands.

Tanya L. Doyle

Mt. Katahdin

I sit upon a rock on top of Katahdin,
Within deep forests rarely trodden,
Gazing on the beauty before me.
I see the sun's bright orange light
Reflecting off the sparkling lake.
I see a magnificent hawk flee
From the summit into its flight,
In its beak, a mouse will never wake.
My eyes take in the incredible view
That is seen by only a few.

John Sidney Smith, IV

Foible

You are a subtle smile
I overlook in my assiduous day.
You are a gentle whisper
I don't try to understand.
Delicate as a dessert,
I devour and fail to taste.

You are as slight as a butterfly,
As fine as a star,
You display in abundance,
Through blinds I see only so far.

I crave to embrace you, to feel you,
Long to set you on high.
Let me see you, hear you,
Rid these blinders from my eyes.

Whisper to me life,
I will listen harder.

Uncover my shade's life,
I will open my mind.

Don't leave me, life,
Until I appreciate your time.

Devyn C. Ascher

Warmly Dressed

A small boy, warmly dressed
Ran out into the snow and was caressed
By its soft and chilling white,
Then got into a snowball fight.

A young lad, bound for school
Plodded through the pristine cool.
With thoughts of classmates on his mind,
He left his footfalls etched behind.

A young man was stalled within his car.
His job awaited him afar.
He could not make his usual trip,
For he was a victim of the winter's grip.

An older man, now retired
Shoveled a pathway through his yard.
The winter to him was a discomforting thing.
His thoughts were on the warmth of spring.

An ancient man through his window peered.
His eyes turned red, then lightly teared.
He remembered he had once been blessed;
He had been a small boy, warmly dressed.

Ed Lahmann

Bedside Sonnet

In her hospital whisper, you're dying.
Her eyes tearing, her long day's breath sour,
Tugging and trembling in the quietest hour.
There, there, like to a baby I'm cooing.
How do I comfort her when I am leaving?
Picture bills stacked on the kitchen counter,
The third hinge—should I remind her now or
Wait to tell her the side gate needs mending?
There, there—my words touch her here,
In this world, and me out, tasting the thought
Of someone comforting her when I'm gone.
Words sink in; I hear myself say, there, there.
Stiffen at the emptiness time has bought,
Staring at the wall, lachrymose with things undone.

Wes Alan Kriesel

Ode to Jack

Halloween has come and gone,
with a nipping chill in the air.
Jack-o-lanterns with sable faces,
perched on porches everywhere.
With each day they get older,
wrinkles casting in their skin;
it commences to shrivel and shrink
until the tops cave in.
The eyes are mournful,
as if they want to cry.
Turning moldy in shades of grey,
they begin to die.
Cracking and falling apart with stress,
the frightful things wouldn't keep.
Scoop them up with a broad shovel,
sling them into the compost heap.
Gathering leaves from left to right,
combing through this autumn mess,
hurling the debits onto the compost pile,
where I laid my Jack to rest.

Walter Clawson

Fallen Children

Do you remember before you were young
When everything was dark and evil,
When all that was here was anger and pure hate?

Now I can only see the tar
Blackening the lit horizons
And the red and orange skies
Ember off into the distance.

They cry as they celebrate the new day rising.
The children of the Four Corners
Bleed on their fallen aspirations.

This is the time now when they will hear our voices
As fallen children shout, "Brotherhood!" in unity.
This is when our fire will begin to glow
Through the candlelit lantern eyes.

Hear the whispers in the night, slowly resonating,
Claiming the hate as their own.
Watch the holy morning turn to nothing,
See the children's fire light up the evening skies.

I can still hear the little lost souls bid,
"Where are we . . ." only to get the patronizing echo "Home . . ."

Nathan R. Phillips

Artist's Profile

Leona Campbell

Quesnel, British Columbia, Canada

I am a survivor! I was diagnosed with cancer at twenty-six and realized how every day is so important. Live each day as it is your last and revel in all it has to offer. I am now forty-seven and my husband was diagnosed with cancer this year. I wrote and dedicated this poem to him, Dennis. I hope by having my poem in print it will help support all others who face the same challenges and help them realize how very important every day of our lives are. Set goals and do the most you can each day, and may all your hopes and dreams come true.

Live for Today

Hey, I see the sunshine
It's such a beautiful day
Would you like a sip of wine
With thanks to him I'll pray
So many mountains left to climb
Only one at a time, we say
And when the golden gates chime
We'll know we earned our stay . . .

Leona Margaret Campbell

rationale

bedspring marks on our backs like tapeworms
i'm a canary in a coal mine
mind stagnant with speed and wine and sex
you move to the next quick-fix
caffeine tea or nicotine lit
i'm just the water you drink with your pills
i am left counting amendments and commandments
you lay, inlaid like ivory
40 proof and waiting for heaven

Jason M. Halla

To Higher Ground

Days in the valley are numbered now.
Children playing in green grass,
Laughing from their bellies, soft, unguarded.
The smell of spring-wet earth,
The faint memory of a dog barking.
I am preparing for the rocky trail upward,
Leaving behind the morning mists
For crystal air cracking against rock surface
To see you on your life journeys.
Sometimes I will smile, sometimes rejoice.
And I know that sometimes I will weep,
Carrying the memory of who you were, once.
You, from the seed of my valley,
Your stories, yet to unfold, not by my design.
I head for high country above the timberline.
And now I make myself light,
Climbing higher than the alpine flowers
To higher ground that meets the night—

Linda Friehling

Artist's Profile

Vinson Hill

New York, New York, USA

I studied with Robert Frost at Dartmouth, who said, "Poetry is a momentary stay against confusion." I enrolled at Juillard, deciding on a music career, especially playing jazz piano and teaching it. While performing in Cape Cod, I discovered the miracle of painting, and became a professional watercolorist specializing in landscapes and lighthouses. I discovered that the different arts' interests reinforced one another. Thus, the poem, "Towards the Lighthouse" was composed. So I, the artist-hunter, attempt to capture the infinite beauty of nature, reinventing its elusive moments and giving them back to be remembered and enjoyed.

Towards the Lighthouse

When the blue
goes out of the water
on late afternoons
lemon foam
and ochre
circle the beach.
I see the lighthouse
in wind grass
green blown
its first light
hovers near
reflecting gulls, starfish
honeysuckle.
I see the light.
I know and become the light
whose finger
presses my mind
breaking and releasing
the dark pyramid
within.

Vinson Hill

Dance of the Moon

The dancing moon glided past my back door.
The moon in all her glory was full of song.
A catchy tune, I began to hum along.
My foot started to tap.
My hips began to groove.
The dance began, I clung to the moon.
We danced across the sky.
The stars watched with a twinkly smile.
The planets moved in perfect time.
The world was my playground—
A chorus full of dreams,
All destined to come true.
One by one they unfolded; the first was you.
A dreamer, I am, who dreamt of finding you.
Little did I know you were friends with the moon.
So now the night brings light in my eyes, song to my heart.
My dreams are for a waking eye because you are mine.

Marie J. Bedell

She's at My Door with Cupcakes

Ain't up to washing dishes
Ain't up to chopping wood
Ain't up to fixin' hinges
I ain't up to no good

I got a rough road to roll
'Cause I'm a tough row to hoe

Like any blues line, baby,
I sing me for all I'm worth
Full of mud and mean and hurt
I've sung since my birth

I got a rough road to roll
'Cause I'm a tough row to hoe

You want to change my tune, watch out!
My beast is heck to slay
My ground is dry and hard as rock
'Cause it ain't rained for days

Richard Lee Martin

Artist's Profile

Franke A. Varca

Houston, Texas, USA

Joshua Clover once said, "The great poetry is written by people who understand there is nothing to be gained from it but the poem itself." The poem, "Boy," speaks of the tender pain of nostalgia, of young fragility, and of who it is we confront every morning in the mirror. It is about what we lose and what we let go and the difference. It has particular personal significance in its relationship to John Berryman and his work, "The Ball Poem." Franke Varca is currently attending college and makes his home in Houston, Texas.

Boy

A boy tosses jacks
as a crowned king
with marble eyes.

Every day from noon to night
he celebrates victories
with plastic tea cups and apple juice.

At times he vanishes into a storm of trees
building forts with palm leaves,
and staking claim to transient clouds.

Bread feeding ducks at a pond
he notices his face
wrinkled by ripples and unfamiliar.

Age, he'll say
much later in his life, was a disease
contracted from thinking too much.

The boy of yesterday
can readily remember only that
the dreaming branches he once swung from
are now a broken betrayal of his past.

Franke A. Varca

Artist's Profile

Lori Weinless Fischler

Brooklyn, New York, USA

This poem is very special to me because it represents an earlier time in my life when the beauty of nature provided the solace, love, and inspiration that I needed. Nature has remained my close companion throughout life. Although everything else in life changes, the beauty and serenity of the natural world has remained constant and has influenced my poetry, photography, and painting. The beauty of nature will continue if we treasure and preserve it. It is our planet's way of showing us love—the major force in the universe that brings us closer to God.

The Game of Chess

A chess game of leaves and twigs
and butterfly wings
on a bark drawn board
was our meeting place.
The sound of water seething
was the music against which
evening dusk fell.

Intent on our game you scarcely noticed
the queen's lavender mantle,
the creeping shadows of the oaks,
the cones thumping
softly against dry leaves.

But I noticed Time, compressed in
a capsule
watching our game,
and heard the buzzing that crickets make
when they converse mid-high
along the water's edge.

Lori Weinless Fischler

Artist's Profile

Lauren Dowless

Copperas Cove, Texas, USA

Roger and I met nine years ago in the spring of 1991. Although we dated for a brief time and we shared a strong, almost spiritual bond, there would be no romance for us. We both knew and accepted the fact that we were just two kindred spirits in search of the one true love. This particular poem is a piece of shared work that I believe shows the intimacy of our spirits. He wrote the first half and left it unfinished. He shared it with me one day, and after reading it, I completed it almost instantly.

Kool Thing

When I am four hundred thought years
from your mind
reach deep and pull me to the surface
of the gray-white jellied jangle of cells.
And for one brief moment,
let me fill all your synapses
with reggae, blues,
and all manner of
strange and wonderful books.
With PMA, passion, and lust,
with affection, tenderness, and
pleasurable pain.
And when I have filled your brain
to orgasmic capacity,
softly, let me slip back
into the depths of your mind
to hauntingly linger
for an eternity.
When I am four hundred thought years
from your mind.

Lauren Dowless and Roger Patterson, Jr.

The Replacement

Her hair is just so . . .
the fiery red setting off against my dull
brown. Pink lipstick in perfect harmony with
the pink of her sweater. Me with my
Chapstick and faded flannel. Her eyes see as
I once did, as I was once allowed; adoration
for you and you alone. And you call her
sweetheart, kiss her in a way you can't
bring yourself to kiss me anymore, although
for so long my lips were your respite, my
kisses your addiction. Replaced by forced,
obliging hugs, there is no greater pain than
an empty caress. My heart swore to only beat
for you, but you beat for another and I now
beat alone. I take the smile out of my
pocket and plaster it on for the passerby
and loved one. I'm fine. I like being
single. I don't mind being replaced.
Hopefully, I'll soon begin to believe myself.

Amy Gardner

Edison the Bus

Dedicated to Luann Waters and The Leopold Education Project

There's a lesson to learn when you see this bus
That God loves us all, even Edison the Bus
June 2000, God sent his angels to the junkyard to
Save and rescue me
God said, I'll fix you up for all the world to see
This spirit in you will bring love, joy,
Happiness, peace, and loyalty
God said, Edison, it's time to pour my spirit
Out all over these schools
You see, Edison, you will be my learning tool
Edison, students will learn about soil and
Water conservation, wildlife
Conservation, solid waste management, agriculture, and forestry
God told Edison: Everywhere you go, people
will also be reminded of Me
Let this be a lesson from Edison the Bus
God loves us all, even Edison the Bus
There is hope with God

Rev. Pam Riddle

Artist's Profile

Mary Komban

Mumbai, India

I am a teacher of natural sciences by profession, but a lover of literature and poetry. In school I was greatly influenced by English poets like Keats, Tennyson, and Wordsworth, and also by Tagore and Sarajoni Naidu of India. I loved to pen poems about all and everything I saw around me. Thus began my sojourn with poetry. "The Ballad of the Tailor's Wife" is a narrative that illustrates the fate of lovers in traditional homes, which inspired me to write the poem with an English background. I hope all enjoy reading it as much as I enjoyed writing it.

The Ballad of the Tailor's Wife

To my husband

The tailor's wife sat a-sewing on the creaky wooden chair
the tunic of her husband that needed mending and care.
He sat by the window tailoring the hem of the most beautiful
wedding dress she'd ever laid eyes upon.
Her dark eyes, they darted now and again to the dress;
it dwelt on its beauty as it grew prettier each step.
"How beautiful!" she sighed, "I wish it had been mine.
I would then have worn it the day I laid my hand in thine."
He looked up with troubled eyes that spoke of a thousand things.
They promised her an easy life, of comfort and pretty things.
"Who, pray thee, is the owner?" she bent low to inquire,
"It's but fair Ophelia's," her husband then did answer.
"Who is the noble suitor?" she queried once again.
"Oh! It's Sir William Woodthroff," her husband then did say.
Her dark eyes then, did fill up with tears, her lips they did quiver.
The tunic left her slender hands, and fell in a heap before her.
For a moment, she had fled far away to her distant lover,
but to be back and never again, never again to her lover.
Now she picked the tunic old that lay in a heap before her,
and sat mending like in the days of old as the twilight drew nearer.

Mary Paul Komban

Impress the Impressers

You are not my Dylan
I am not your Sandburg
I am not the lips that will kill the fire
You can never be the heated courage won
Candid fortunate sons and songs be undone
Living will never tell, but this:
You cannot impress the impressers

Warring lives converge
Painted jealousy strikes
Loving that which gives
Red deserted hands hit
Your undisputed dirge
But you cannot impress the impressers

The dead is past
The train has moved on
The Impressers have to smile
"We are not easily won," they say
And you cannot impress the impressers
Try Colonel Tom—I will take you on
You cannot impress the impressers

Brett McCauley Greene

The Death of Anne Frank

You were impossibly young
To hang limp, bruised, starving
On the edge of a barbed wire fence

You, with your brown hair,
Your cinnamon eyes, your sacred
Grin of wonder and belief

To call to a friend you remember
From school
To call to her through the ash-laden
Air
Through the wires, passed the turrets

"Is that you?"

"Yes, Anne, it's me."

"Yes, it's me," the guard intervenes,
"It's me," he jests, "It's me."

And so, in a whiplash of seconds
You are flying, Anne,
You are soaring
You're a star
A star

Nicolle Ann Joyce

Artist's Profile

Patrice Cathey

Amherst, New York, USA

Patrice Cathey is a performance poet who performs with live jazz accompaniment utilizing the upright bass, keyboards, and flute. Her poems express high levels of emotion, and usually speak of relationships, be they positive or negative. She is an educator, and the founder of Poetically Speaking Poetry Worships for Children. This organization introduces children to the joys of poetry coupled with visual artistic expression. "Perhaps Virginia" is a blueprint for the future, and encompasses what we have learned from the past. It is a whisper of what was lost, and still propels a shout of joy for what can still be.

Perhaps Virginia

I cannot hold tightly to an iceberg
My hands will grow cold, my heart will freeze
Making it impossible to love
My lips will grow numb and I will not be able
To feel the tenderness of your kiss

Instead I need a warm man with a warm heart
Who is able to fill me with the glow
Of the noontime sun
And ignite my blood with the richness of
Red wine and sparkling brandy

And I will not waste another lifetime
Attempting to warm a loveless iceberg
For he would then melt away
And become less of what he aspires to be

I will instead walk away from the arctic
Moving in a southerly direction
With my heart facing the sun
In search of a glimmer of the warmth awaiting me

Perhaps . . . Virginia

Patrice Cathey

Dosimeter

The waves crash upon the beach . . .

"I am tainted," I hear as he smashed through
the sand and into a dream. . . .

The stars screamed with rage as I plucked
the melons from the water, setting them free.
"Come with me," says the fisherman.
I walk with myself.

The sailor spies the lowly creature,
and crushes the oyster upon the rocks.
Revenge is tearful on this sad, forlorn shore. . . .

Farewell my friend.

David Butler

Thoughts from a Moving Train

The buildings are old and desolate
Faded factories and worn-out mills
Landfills now overgrown
Covered in swamp life
Marsh and polluted muck
"Private Property!" the signs scream
As if someone were really interested in listening
As if someone really cared to tread there
Grease and oil floating in murky water
And if I look carefully
If you watch ever so closely
You can see the sun
Reflect its golden halo
From the window behind
And shower its golden rain spell
So that for just—one moment
You can almost see Nirvana
Between God's tears

Tamitha Darling

two weeks 'til spring

the eerie moonlit snowscape
hollows her burgundy room
we sit eye to eye
separated by hundreds of miles
of fear and mutual gloom

the golden paint of the molding
seems so very misplaced
a cheerful reminder that
our lives so rapidly change
into fear and distaste

gazing away
i dream, she cries
of the coming spring
and a long ride to madison

her white, french-cuffed shirt
speaks now of our mounting mistakes
she is camouflaged depravity
i've funded the fall
with fear and insatiable need

Chad Spencer Anauo

Time Flies

The clock taxied in
the runaway. I gave the hourglass
my ticket and to my
seat on the minute hands.
No complimentary peanuts, please.
A voice, "Now departing for
six o'clock and beyond.
Please fasten your watches."
A glide, a bump, we're off!
I watch out the window as
we soar past mid-morning
and lunchtime.
We have reached afternoon when
the on-flight
movie has ended.
We are exiting the clock.
I snatch my carry-on
baggage of hope and dreams
for the future and stride
away.

Lauren Sillery

Artist's Profile

Eileen McGrath

Newbury Park, California, USA

This poem is dedicated to my mother, Dorothy Jane (Rigney) Reilly, who still longs for "a house of her own." She was born January 20, 1910, in Rensselaer, New York, and sent to live in an orphanage at eight years of age and a sanatorium for tuberculosis at twelve. Finally, she went to Nellie's rooming house until marriage to my father. Mommy shared a home with her husband of fifty-four years, their eight children, and her sister Marion. This is "a poem of her own," a glimpse from her childhood.

Mommy's Hearse

Today I ride alone
clip-clop down cobblestone streets
slick with rain.
Cold black wind echoes dark pain
swirls within my head.

Today I see her
through drops on the glass.
She lies in that coach.
She'll never, never go too far.
See, she's there just up ahead.

Yesterday warm against her breast
soft smells of roses, colorful petals eager to dance
laugh and play together in my head.

Alone on the porch, dusk has come.
She'll never, never leave me.
I'm only eight!
I'll sit and wait and wait.

Grandmother whispers,
"Come, Dorothy, it's time for bed."

Eileen McGrath

The Dance

The leaves,
though they're dying,
still believe they are flying.
They soar,
taste the wind, paint the ground, scent the air.
The fall leaves abound.
They fall all around,
and I dance the season
among them for now.
I dance for the voyage that this bright Earth has made.
I dance for the Mother Sun, steadfast in her stay.
I dance for the rhythm that this world can't mandate.
I dance for the journey that I too must take.
The dressed autumn leaves,
they play their lament.
They make it a melody on their last descent.
I can't sing along for I know not their song,
But I'll dance 'til their melody ends. Yes,
I must dance 'til the melody ends.

Julia Graham

Saipan Flashback

Scarlet bougainvillea trailing down the wall
like drops of blood, veils a gutted hut
rotting in the corner of a ravaged yard.

Showering golden blossoms,
the remnant of a tree survives beside the pool
where once young lovers met, loved, coupled.

A vanished infant's shoe molders near a broken toy
screaming out in silence.

And rusting in the surf
crippled landing craft
scar a sandy shore.

Phyllis J. Favors

Artist's Profile

Andrea L. B. Bowman

Sherwood, Oregon, USA

"Writing is water for a parched soul." I have been writing poetry since I was ten years old. Some have called it a gift; it is one I am happy to share. I find it is more a way to emphasize the good in my life, and to make the not-so-good positive. It is a form of perseverance. My poetry comforts and uplifts me, allows me to express my innermost feelings, and explore my nature and spirituality. Each poem is very close to my heart. I write because my heart has something to say.

Vanity

Graceful maples,
tired of their anonymous green tresses,
on a whim
dye themselves shades
of ruby red and sunwashed gold.
But, oh, what a pity!
It seems the dye
has damaged the roots
of their resplendent manes.
Their colored crowns
come out in clumps,
leaving the maples
crying tears of syrup,
naked and bald.

Andrea L. B. Bowman

Our Kisses Are Only Blown

Our kisses are only blown,
caught between the sea,
a vision from a distance;
I can't see you, and you can't see me.

I can feel the wind move across my skin,
an ever soft touch and grace.
I can feel that you are here,
but why is there such a space?

The gap is very wide;
when will we meet in the middle?
The love we feel is a trap;
why can't it be easy and simple?

I long for a human embrace,
I want our love to be shown.
The feelings we have will meet someday;
until then, our kisses are only blown.

Katie Pickard

The Cycle

She's screaming out to her child
In her own language
This is all her native tongue
She recognizes this all from her own past
She's repeating the steps her parents took
And she doesn't even realize it
And does she care
She's beating her own child down
An innocent child
Her own flesh and blood
Does she realize that she's repeating the cycle
She's repeating the same evil
Blood dripping words as her own abusers did
She's looking at her own child with such a rage
Looks at her own baby with such malice and hate
And beats her down
Will this cycle ever end

Ariane Seifert

Artist's Profile

Natalya Marian Brettle

Edmonton, Alberta, Canada

I am an English major at the University of Alberta. I have been writing poetry prolifically from a young age and have high hopes for the future. Currently, my strongest influence is the modernist movement of the early twentieth century, particularly Ezra Pound and his circle. I believe that young, innovative poets of the twenty-first century can learn much from their style and technique. I wanted to write a "pastoral" poem as a testament to the human spirit's enduring love for nature and the simpler things in life, even in our growing urban landscape where technology is king.

Birch Bark

The lazy girl!
She's as sensual as birch bark!
She doesn't sashay. She struts and glides.
She struts and glides right into trouble
Every time.
Every time she raises her eyes,
She says something to surprise. . . .
She spent her days
In a reverie of pleasantries,
Lolling on the luscious hills,
Communing with the peasantry.
She has a voluptuous sense of serenity
As she basks in the decadence
Of her willful heart. . . .
She spends her days
Breaking bread on the luscious hills.
That lazy girl!
She's as sensual as birch bark!
In a reverie of pleasantries,
Communing with the peasantry.

Natalya Marian Brettle

Artist's Profile

Jennifer Lauren Griffith

Tuscaloosa, Alabama, USA

Poetry, to me, is a good medicine. I have discovered it to be a way to express whatever I am going through at the moment. All my life I thought I would be an Olympic swimmer. When I tore my rotator cuff at fourteen years of age, all those dreams were shattered. In this poem, I looked back at what it felt like to do something I loved. Writing this poem allowed me to remember my passion, and not to focus on the bitterness of losing my dream.

Religious Experience

Off the block
My body tears through
Plunging toward the bottom
I ride the crest to the surface
Stroking, splashing
I connect with an underworld
Dead bugs in the drain
Broken, black tiles
Seething stench of chlorine
Cheers and screams are muffled down there
Only sounds of pulsing liquid
Some have gone all the way down
Initials and dates
Scratched into muted blue concrete
Abandoned pennies
Forming permanent copper cameos
A solitary sanctuary
Where my chest burns
Lungs long for oxygen
Two more pulls to the wall—I will not take a breath.

Jennifer Lauren Griffith

The Marble Fountain

In a courtyard of aged stone
Where the ivy crawls in twisted ways
Covering the brick is green hair of an unhappy clown
Moving and turning in ways not ordinary to common life
In the center of this room
A statue juts from the crumbling rock
A marble carving
Adonis to the world
It sits and dances
Yet frozen to the eye
Beams of sun are pulled down from the air
Reflect and shimmer off the icy pool
Drops of lost and weeping liquid
Seep from a crack in the marble bowl
Crystal sadness drips
Tears of a pouting angel
They glisten for a moment then disappear
Drip drop
Pitter pat
Thickening the soft moss below

Stosh Michael Konopacki

Falling

What strange and wonderful human
Error
Caused the door to tear open at 30,000 feet—
She thought.
The pretty young woman with
Perfectly manicured face
Floats through the opening
As a princess enters a ball—falling.
The blue folds of her dress give up
Their stiffness and
Billow up softly around her.
She admires the gracelessness
And lightness of her limbs akimbo.
Eyes wide in wonderment,
Wind whipping her earthbound—falling.
She looks dispassionately at her sky home
Become a silver speck
Resigned to her certain descent—
Amused that there will be such a sloppy end
To her precise life—falling.

Sara Elizabeth Kaufman

Pandora and I

Pandora and I . . .
Foolish children of wonder
One myth, one flesh,
Both destined for the scapegoat's curse.

Pandora and I . . .
Created as catastrophic gifts,
Bestowed, it would seem, as doom to many,
But the casualty has been "Self."

Self-deception, self-destruction, self-conviction,
Sentence passed.

Born of imagination, ideals, and illusion,
Tragic inventions of the "society of gods,"
Our forced folly has been our demise;
Mischief has opened the "box of blame."

Pandora and I . . .
My shadow, myself,
Misconceptions further our resemblance;
All the talents given only to deceive
Leave a legacy of disaster ever after.

Connie Whitney

Untitled

All I have to give
is myself
as I am
take it or
leave it
I'll pretend
I don't care

Siobhan McFadden

Artist's Profile

Kelly R. Rowe

Sacramento, California, USA

This poem is an expression of who I am. It is hard to express what growing up feels like on the inside. The only way I ever felt safe expressing my innermost thoughts is in writing. My mother taught me that when something is on your mind, writing it down in some fashion is a wonderful way to release it. This is only one of the reasons I will always love her so much.

My Definition

The candle glowing bright in the kitchen
Lights up the entire room.
The hum of the refrigerator running its own course
Is the only break in the penetrating silence,
Which defines who I am.
A girl not yet sure if she is a woman,
Lost inside her own flickering scattered thoughts.
Once great ideas turned into fading fantasies,
Locked down deep inside her own personal dungeon.
The few who escape their prison are pushed forward
Without complete confidence.
Breaking free into the beautiful shining sunlight,
Some are held dear and flourish,
While others are spooked by fear and left for dead.
I am a young lady slowly gaining balance within her own mind.
Growing up is much more than a physical process.
Like the body, the mind must be allowed to run its own natural course.
The scrunched thoughts and ideas cramped inside my head,
Fighting to straighten themselves out,
Are what truly define who I am.

Kelly R. Rowe

Don't Go to Florida and Leave Me Here

Don't go to Florida and leave me here,
as the weatherman shadows your whole state
into darkness with one hand;
he says that the climate will be lukewarm
like a puddle.
I am drinking in a country bar,
listening to cowboys sing old Merle Haggard
songs as the TV blares an ad for Disneyworld.
I have been left for a lukewarm mouse,
not even singing "The Rose" pressed
against "Big Abe's" belly seems comforting.
I am a pink-haired, tattooed lesbian in a room
full of Texas-loving sons of Uncle Sam.
I am waiting to be killed,
then I can prove you were wrong for leaving.
My head hangs over my scotch;
they only tip ten gallons of pride at me.
I am more pathetic than any of the drunkards
in this room.

Lyska S. Mondor

Prayer to the Rain God

Oh, hard rain that drums on the tin eaves,
Smacks the blacktop with nonstop splattering,
Raps the window glass with each wind gust,
And spouts out the drainpipe an artesian spring;
Oh, anti-liturgical benediction;
Oh, rampant and wanton redemption;
Oh, most holy gully-washer and moisture-laden westerly offshore flow:

Make frothing brooks in the dry ditches
And roiling creek beds out of rock-strewn arroyos.
Swell the stream to a leaping, swirling, dusky rush,
And let it billow out a silt cloud into the big river.
Drench all desire and longing,
All pleasure and depression,
All scheming and regret,
Be they solitary leaf or uprooted tree,
And, in the wild ebullient overflow,
Sweep them out to sea.

John Williams

Artist's Profile

Donora Hillard

Shavertown, Pennsylvania, USA

My poem describes a relationship with an older man; the title refers to an ancient Phoenician God to whom children were sacrificed by burning. This poem hits home on many levels, which is what writing at its best should do. Written expression, I feel, is the supreme elucidator for innermost thoughts and feelings. Through poetry you can "cry out loud the soul's own secret joy" or give closure to that which would otherwise fester.

Moloch

Before I met you I
Did not exist you
Say and I
Begin to believe it.

Lost in the circadian
Rhythm of you
Above and me
Beneath and I
Sometimes have words delinquent.

Not feeling deserving you
Are so damn good with expression and
Though I leave you tumescent I
Lack the strength and
Soul to cease.

Donora Hillard

Fortune

As she files my nails she talks about herself,
Her six year-old daughter,
Her escape from Vietnam,
Her family
Rich enough to send her here
To escape the chaos.

She was ten.
Old enough
To take her younger brother.
A child raising a child.

By eighteen
Raising another.

She wants to get married;
"Husband bring me happiness."
But she doesn't expect anyone to ask.
She says she is too skinny,
And looks like a boy.

I interrupt to tell her I would kill for her figure.
She stares at me, and then smiles.
She says a fortune teller once told her she would be rich by thirty.

Nancy Castaneda

Monsoon

Each afternoon as the temperature
climbs into the hundreds,
I bloom. Rich and fragrant, deep colors
vibrant against the parched earth.
My life undulates like meringue on a pie I once baked for a man
who had no sweet tooth.

Dusty memories stir as I stand alone
against the darkening sky,
anticipating the rain.

Phyllis D. Weston

Art of Gaucherie

Stumbling upon an art form,
the lead and ink
flow onto the pulp of creation.
A plethora of nigrescence
furthers its absence as
the clearest of ideas tames
the most feral of entities:
the mind.
Control no longer a trepidation,
the images painted with such ineptness
now contrive blueprints for appreciation.
It is on this very plane that the
wooden wand conjures up its most
basic and purest of splendors.
The artist merely a puppet
reacting to the stringy antics
of the quill.
Stumbling as he may . . . however,
discovering a gift of gracefulness.

Joseph Donald Teague

Ave de Champ E'lysees, Late Summer, 1999

Hemingway has gone away
and taken Paris with him.

I'd walked the streets for days and found
nothing
—save the absolute perfect croissant
with chocolate studs like jewels—
that could convince me I was in
an old world den of culture.

I went to McDonald's to see if they really
called them
Royales with cheese.
They did,
but that joke wore thin on Mickey D's #43
as I sat out front drinking coffee
in the lengthening shadow of glory
and triumph.

Charles Reed

Artist's Profile

Luke Morvant

Arcadia, California, USA

While I have written many haikus, the one I have selected, "The Oscillation of Alaska," is the most significant. You see, many of my poems are based on my memories, and this one is no exception. It was not until I moved away from Alaska, the place I spent the first eleven years of life, that I began to appreciate the changing of the seasons or how I will always remember them, from outside of my window.

The Oscillation of Alaska
(A Three-Haiku Poem)

A season visits
Today, a vision of snow
The plains hibernate.

Snow season has come
A white vision delivered
The plains' new portrait.

Nomadic season
The snow moves on to new lands
The plains awaken.

Luke Morvant

My Girl

I still remember that long, lonely road
Ten months and ten days long.
At the end you arrived,
Piercing through my womb,
Clenched fists drenched in blood.
Grandmothers wept, grandfathers spat.
Well-wishers hung sad charcoals on the front door.
"It's a girl!"
Only I smiled, because I knew.
The sweat of my sweat covered your body
When the sun drilled through my pores
In the brick kiln, the rice fields,
Endless realms of my burden.
Your blood sprang with every dirty touch
I endured.
Now, when you start walking this earth
On your wobbly feet,
You will know exactly which door to walk in to.

Arna Seal

The Farmer

As long as he contends with dirt
Crumbles and breezes found in dust,
History is the row of grapes
Lying straight down the dimpled hill, becoming.
The future fuses to the sunshine
Sweating down his back,
Arched with satisfied muscle, tanning.
Alone the day, night must be
Peopled with reflection,
Or do views from porches finally develop into views?
Longing must turn around the trellis, the captured chase of buds
A slowed tear,
Or do eyes wander to the roadway, now and then,
Anticipating the long black car of letters,
Jumping behind themselves to: come for me?

Sip of Coke and back inside
I bustle, rendering the wrinkled Mexican
A farmer once again.

Rider Strong

Wait for You

You said it will only be a few days. . . .

I counted the fingers on my left
then my right hand
then once again, and once again

Spring bloomed all around me
like the flowers on the caressing sheets
that comforted me each night

Summer burned with the moist air of sleepless
visions long and countless, hot and restless

Fall ripened our bed with blankets
like the growing red peas beneath the Ormosia
round, solid, and delicious.
The Chinese called them "love peas"
for thousands of years.

Winter whispered purity
beneath the blankets of snow and promises

Tonight, as I climbed into bed
alone
I left the light on for you
again.

Guili Zhang

Inching

Moments like this flicker
Like a candle at the seashore.
We did not know how long it would last.

There they were: embraced,
Moving side to side
On the embankment
That overlooks the interstate.

The long grass tickled my mother's knees;
My father's cheek grew red.

They spoke in whispers
That the sweeping clouds enveloped
And stole away from us.

Their quiet moment:
Disturbed only by the
Gaze of two small daughters
As we got closer.

We were inching,
Climbing higher up the hill
To get a better look.

Jessica Anthony

Artist's Profile

Susan E. Spencer

Brighton, Massachusetts, USA

Every word I have written or will ever write is the product of my parents' undying love and faith in all that I do. They have never given up on me and have never allowed me to give up on myself. My words are derived from their inspiration. They taught me everything I know, I write only what I know. They are my greater gods and I am merely their plagiarist. They inspire me to be more.

The Original Plagiarist

My wisdom spans o'er thousands of years
Genres generated from greater Gods
But do not bid me your generous cheer
The fool be you to place on me your odds.
I sound the barbaric YAWP of Whitman.
On the roofs of the world I paint my lie
To Van Gogh, Cezanne, Seurat, and Gauguin
Play on music and so sicken and die!
Alas 'tis true, I have gone here and there
My muses do range from ancient to peers
But do not mock me for the secrets I share,
How would I greet thee? With silence and tears.

Before you judge, one more for you to hear,
The title's lent from a friend I hold dear!

Susan E. Spencer

Artist's Profile

Ruth B. Rauth

Terrace Park, Ohio, USA

Ruth Binkley Rauth is a journalist whose poems have won prizes and been published in many periodicals. She has been visiting poet in the school's poetry workshop, coordinator, judge, sponsor of contests, and leader of Life Rhythms classes at a retirement center. An active member of the Greatest Cincinnati Writer's League and past Vice President of the Ohio Poetry Association, she also belongs to the National Federation of State Poetry Societies and has twice partici-pated in the Antioch Writer's Workshops. Growing up in a family of nature lovers who also loved to play word games, Ruth began early to "paint word pictures." Her three sons and grandsons have provided the inspiration for some of her poems, as have persons who have shared their life stories.

Of Time and Dreams

Father's gold pocket watch measured heartbeats,
times for surgery and the slow drip of an IV.
All else in his life was overture
to main events, like birth and death
of those the family never knew.

Steps from my childhood dreams to his were counted
in places where treasures were wet pebbles
and the pulse of life was seen in raindrops on the lake.

Now the watch is mine, and I yearn to throw it,
like a pebble into the past,
to see it skip and yield to places we never shared,
like blue-green eddies near the shore
and grasses curled by the wind.

Yet, warming in my palm, this measurer of his days
seems to sing the music of turning points
where drying dreams meet others born anew,
emerging through images of caring,
to rhythms more than metrical
that I've yet to understand.

Ruth B. Rauth

Island House

It's cool here tonight;
much too cool for this time of year.
Makes me remember the December I moved here.
A week before Christmas—
all I had was a wicker chest,
a Christmas tree, and you.
I played my music much too loud that season,
drank too much wine, ignored all the reasons
I should be kinder to myself,
made believe the love we made
was enough.
Here I am again—a lifetime later—
letting the coolness and the breeze
stir your sleeping ghost—
missing your humor most,
still crying over milk that was never spilled.

Joanne Carlton Humphries

A Fly in Amber

Little immortal
of a bygone age
caught
in the act of living.
Sleek, black body
with silver wings,
about to fly
in a world of golden crystal.
You are the messenger
of the time
that used to be,
a quiet echo
of vanished, ancient seas.
Only your beauty is left,
but that is quite enough
for us,
who will be only dust,
instead of amber beauty.

Peter DeLellis

Plaid Shorts and Black Coffee

Sitting to the back of the improper cafe,
I stare at my old black coffee.
Staring, feeling like plaid shorts in the center of Times Square.
Plaid shorts, hanging, from the commercial apple
falling to its last second.
In the door the "propers" come, they stare
for a moment, I wonder. A moment is all,
for the slick of the coffee holds more appeal.
Staring to the bottomless whole, I realized plaid shorts
are more alive than the Monday-through-Friday
Oxford attitude will ever be.

Patrick Michael Rice

The Dancer

Good morning, Mother Sun, did you sleep well?
You look rested and bright this morning,
arriving with such a colorful display.

Your husband's work last night was wonderful,
though he was upstaged by the stars
until the fog took its seat in the balcony.

You two are a funny couple,
modern in your parenting arrangement.
With his insomnia, it is only natural,
him watching the children while they sleep.

I am always inspired by the pas des deux
when he glows on the edge of the stage,
while you hover above the symphony pit
in your brilliant act of illumination.

Do you tire, Mother? You're beginning to sink.
Will you indulge us with a colorful finale?
Ah, the prima donna, you captivate us.
A breathtaking performance, graceful curtsy,
you disappear behind a black velvet horizon.

But never a curtain call, how hard we clap.

Rea J. Fraser

Artist's Profile

Thomas Kim

Lawrenceville, New Jersey, USA

I've found that I have become a deep-seated social commentator. Originally a graphic artist, I have morphed through several different forms of creative, passionate expression, including dancing, music production, and rapping. Unlike the usual art student, I am finishing up an education in business school. Although it may not be seen as a contribution to my artwork, I have found that money transcends across all subject matters of life, giving me a unique perspective as an artist.

Consumer Culture

Years of increasing depressants
slow down adolescents
and the signs of effervescence
clears like the top
of a 7-Up drop
that sparkles and tingles
in your teeth
but the slippery sweet of a toffee Heath
completes my independence

Thomas S. Kim

Daddy's Land

My kinsfolk bathed
in soaps of ground corn grits,
cleansed their teeth with birch reed,
sifted galax leaves by reticent light.
Grandpa laid creek rock in timeworn well,
killed a hog every November.
On Daddy's land out in the trailer
cousin Danny blew out his brains.

Mama knocked my sister
plumb across the kitchen.

Barbara of Brushy Fork,
I turned my gaze, your blemished face,
I heard your immeasurable tale.
You, who worked the glove factory
for a dollar twenty-five in '68,
leave your wilted heart to bloodroot,
your hemp sacks to the millwright.

Nubbins from the corncrib of Appalachia,
clothes on the beating block,
there resides a closeted people.

Annehart Herrick

Think Back

It is unlikely now that you will recall
burning your forehead on a heated
asphalt afternoon while you ran
for survival
bearing your courage
grinding it on the limestone of humanity
Your past is tacked in a recess—embedded—
a necropolis of half smiles
shaded from an elusive warmth
you cringe at
remembering haltingly
your hopes
dreams singeing the soul
like crescent points
You will try to jerk it out
with vehement shakes
flicker your moods in pensive vitriol
drink from the future
dousing pretence over the shadow
of your former self

Prerna Rajen Desai

Another Mystery

When the sky is the color
of emeralds and oceans
at 5:55 a.m. (another mystery)
I will experiment with form.
I will shape-shift to become an elephant
and I will scream at mice
and trample the masses
and worship peanuts.
I will become a field of tulips
lovers' tears
burning red desire
the crunch of metal
passed from mouth to mouth.
But I will stay here at 5:55 a.m.
another mystery
until it passes and becomes
just 5:56.

Toby Levin

Transatlantic Cancer

She was always my grandfather's daughter
on the floor of the living room at daybreak
with her legs stretched out in West Germany.
A saltwater swelling was whispering:
(It bloomed in his lungs like a day lily
that afternoon on the gingham couch
next to his wife.
And in the evening the silver hair and
blue wool hung onto his body
like sweat on a forehead.)
Nourish this tired heart.
He was not,
and the stereo played
a tape of his funeral in North America.
I was
in the adjacent room
while my headphones blared
something about my love being the size of the tumors inside of us.

Megan Alena Ziesmer

Where Can You Find Your Future?

The future is a Polaroid
picture sitting in your palm
waiting to develop

Some have the choice
of smudging it with their fingers
or preserving it with their eyes

Some wait so long
and fill up with anticipation
just to find it isn't what they want

It is but a black sheet
of nothing
but wasted anticipation

Jessie Marie Burkholder

The Dry Land

A soft comfort on a cold bus
and Arizona passes me by.
The fake desert of cow-grass and brown
misleads from the sky.
Abandoned hills give home
to the sunset of sweet orange
and an indescribable glow
to which I am now so much closer.
The canyon in its grandeur
truly is a mystic:
an overwhelming beast
not tangible, touchable,
but there just the same.
And Sedona with her red earth,
pushed upward toward the sky
shows in all her glory
how Mother Nature is kind.

Jordan Leigh Scott

Artist's Profile

Pin Quan Ng

Singapore, Singapore

"You know why I'll always be a lousy writer? Because nothing ever happens in my life; that's why." That's what I told my best friend, Choo Zhengxi. In short, I make no pretensions to being an artist, but I keep writing anyway. I'd first like to acknowledge Ms. Wong Piechi and Ms. Grace Chua; they took the time to properly educate me. I dare say you're my Professor Higgins and Colonel Pickering, girls. I want to thank my mentor, Ms. Ho Pohfun, for believing in me and seeing what others didn't. Finally, I give thanks to Muses Peich, Hu Peilin, Judith Huang, Jacqueline Tang, and Andrea Chin; they have all been sources of inspiration.

sourgrapes

some live to eat; i'd die to
taste those laudanum lips
wipe off that saccharine smile
savour a slice of cherry pie
with a glass of bloody virgin mary

hershey's kisses seem teardrops
bittersweet but
swallowed pride; pills; preservatives prevent
having the wedding cake and eating it
too much chocolate is bad
valentine candy carcinogenic
anathema to anorexia

her tongue is sucrose sharp
and i take my tea black
she'll eat those
words; put in my mouth
i've had the milk; it was sour
why buy the cow? to have steak

Pin Quan Ng

Rita

As an Oklahoma autumn advanced
You stood at the door of the pickup
You pronounced the end of summer

I saw behind you
The thunder blue sky
A car park of rain pools

I knew you were wise
I wished you would be mine

John McLester

unpacking

eighty-five degrees at 11:15
unpacking the last of my mother's furniture
in the dark, humid stillness
cutting past the Minnesota return address
in her neat school teacher printing
through the outer-box

there, nestled in six inches of foam peanuts
and three layers of bubble wrap
is the mahogany bookshelf
that stood in our front room for seventy-five years

pulling it out
the peanuts swirl and eddy at my feet
a foam snow in this hot climate
these memories drift deep
and dark as mahogany

Virginia H. Ward

Artist's Profile

Stacy D. Zorn

Willow Springs, Missouri, USA

One of my first loves is to write poetry. I have spent most of my life in the southern region of Missouri, which is part of the Ozarks. My family moved to the area when I was fifteen, and, even at that tender age, I knew I was somewhere special. The forests and the streams are amazing, and I have become an avid nature lover. My family spends a lot of time canoeing and hiking. I have experienced great success in business, but there are two things in life that are more fulfilling to me: Family and writing. I have a wonderful son who is entirely too energetic, but very smart and a lot of fun. My husband is warm and supportive of everything I do. As for my writing, I have written poetry since elementary school. I find it is the best release I have for anything life presents.

Longing

I long to be in Memphis
dining with the royal Peabody ducks
and playing the piano player
with the sexy goatee, who
pounds the flat black keys
until they swell and scream.
I long to be where puppets
dance to the blues, and
muddy water inhales itself
into varied spinning swirls
(muddy like my name when I return home).
My heart throbs for Memphis,
for my desire—the piano player, perhaps.
For the sweet smell of beer
on the sidewalk at midnight,
muddy swirls, and fat greasy girls.
For sweaty street singers, performers,
players with voices and faces of cherubs.

Stacy D. Zorn

A Gathering of Limbs

Gathering branches in the snow
Outside the city walls, we build
Fires in coal-pits beside broken tracks.
Our torn gloves are stiffened
With blood. Worn garments are hung
Upon our backs.

From the sky and shadows—blue and black—
A creature stirred,
Emerged.
It stared at twenty ripped hands
Clutching ten spears,
Then resigned.

And when the shadows subside
The bruise resides.
We trudge in the glare
Over blood and dirt blessed in snow
Towards glaciers we cannot pass.

Christopher Black

Waiting for Morning

Grandpa had been fishing all night
When he came home to find
A note that explained nothing
The perfect house explained it all
Grandma was hanging in the garage
In her favorite blue dress

I spent the night there two months later
Sleep interrupted
By the old grandfather clock
Playing music on the hour
Chimes on the half-hour
Ghosts never sleep
(Not for children)
Jumping to my feet
I split my shin on the bed rail
A cut that never healed quite right

Stephen Craig Smith

Artist's Profile

Mei Mei Chui

Brooklyn, New York, USA

My life was an empty vase. Poetry is a fragment of the vase. I was born in 1979 in New York City. I met my father for the first time when I was nine. After I had lived in Hong Kong for twelve years, my family and I came to the U.S. My academic major and minor are law and English, respectively. I have been in love with poetry since the summer of 2000. I love art, music, and literature. I believe in humanity.

Love Me . . .

I am so foolish and naive—I must have
forgotten—shattered glass does hurt. I
once more reach my bare hands, naked fingers
trying to mend the shattered glass;
the pieces sparkling and shining—
the ocean in sunset—the pieces
sparkling and shining—the starry firmament.
A touch, a grasp, a shrill chill
rouses me from my peaceful sleep . . .
blood-red tears pouring out from the wounds,
deep down from the phalanges
of every finger tip, finger-pad,
finger-joint of my thumbs, index, middle,
ring, and little fingers; of the balls of
the thumb; from the cuttings of the head,
heart, and life lines
falling apart on my palms—
the inflaming magma flooding,
running down, overwhelms the veins
in every part of my body—pain. . . .

Mei Mei Chui

Artist's Profile

Jen Puff

Allendale, Michigan, USA

I was born and raised in Newaygo. For me, poetry is a way of venting my feelings. I write my best poetry when I am emotional. My advice to others interested in writing is to . . . write. Write what you are feeling. That is what makes the best poetry. Write from your heart and, no matter what, you will have success.

Picking Up the Pieces

The day has not started. The sun is not
yet awake, but they are, tiptoeing through
the house like a little band of elves. Picking
up a lamp here. Turning over a chair there.
Two in the living room sweeping up what
used to be the window. Broken dishes are
quickly put into garbage bags. The dining
room chair with the now missing leg is
hidden carefully in the garage. One on
hands and knees scrubbing blood spots
off the floor hoping no one will know. The
routine is known by heart and nearly has
its own calendar square. The same
thought runs through their heads. "If we do
it better, things will get better." But in their
hearts they know. It will never be good
enough and it will never end.

Jen Ann Puff

Artist's Profile

J. Wick

Newton, Iowa, USA

This selection is actually part one of a two part template and the body was edited specifically for entry. I use poems like these to generate lyric ideas of which the finished product is a song. Of this particular poem, only six lines were kept for the song. Some lines are doubled, others branch off into different, but related ideas. To this date, the song is unfinished, but close. Who knows how many changes are made before the writer is satisfied and can say, "It is finished." I enjoyed writing this. I hope you enjoy reading it.

Old Songs and Bellyaches

Gotta get up outta here to talk around,
Stretch my legs and look the clown—hermit.
Stop! Looking out this window no one can look into,
Nothing is so permanent as ink inside your skin. You
Can't wait to leave this vehicle stolen;
You drove into town loaded to the ground.
Through this house with everybody sleeping,
My moves feel so loud as I cannot make a sound.
You can hear it when I finally fall asleep.
A musical dream, it's no longer about me anymore.
Walking through every spider's web,
This ebbs faster than my life. Which comes first:
The idea of death or the egg?
I came, I wanted to tell you, "I love you," but
I just forget some days; the feeling's there,
It's all through here just the same.
Not really forgetting old songs, been working on
Remembering sing-a-longs:
Get on with it! Get over it!
As actions catch up with thinking, you're lady luck.

J. Wick

People

My darling counterpoint
who steals the sheets
from my side of the universe

has tossed aside
those mightier than he
to swing chandelier-bright
above the flames in my head,

blazing in a broad guffaw
and entertaining as any good
embargo, but, oh!

all stars, all halos he,
curled under my arm like a seed.

Hamil Rasihovich Hamaev

Cancer

I once lived for eight years without sorrow. I know now that it
will never go away. Every day is a new beginning, a new fight,
a new struggle to not only maintain my sanity but my empathy . . .
as well. I have learned the way just as many times as I have
followed the path, and yet I gain nothing: no insight, no pain,
no sorrow, not even a glimpse
of the beginning and nowhere in sight do I find the end.
I have listened to me tell myself this
over and over again and have yet to realize the severity of what
the problem is, and, even worse, to find a way out
seems like just another faint dream that is endorsed by everything
and everyone in this world.
The world, itself, is not the problem,
and that notion is the faint dream of my life hung upon the
window of kindness through which
the light of redemption
shines through to clarify and filter into 100% truth—and that's that.
I am the problem, and I am my own insight and sadness,
and I am the only one who has a glimpse to the beginning
and knows that there will be an end.

Jason William Wyatt

Before Life

You are tired.
You always are
when we finish.
I can't sleep, as usual,
so I turn and, hanging
my feet from the side
of the bed, place
my head on your flat stomach
and just feel you sleep, feel
you breathe. I will do this
every night for the next
nine months,
and while I won't be sure
for three more weeks,
I know I hear,
I feel two hearts,
two breaths.

Jesse A. Minneman

Simple Pleasures

On your knee, in the lamplight
dipping buttered toast in your coffee,
I hear the hush of the silent house.
The other children gone off to school,
you and I sit together
alone in the dim morning light
full of love and trust
chattering to one another about
simple times with unfurrowed brows.
We were so close then.
I hold that memory in my mind
like an old black and white photograph
one would carry in a wallet worn soft
from years of riding in a back pocket—
a photo
showing the ones you love
the most beautiful mother,
the best loved and dearest held,
the treasured one
to be shown far from home.

Mollie R. Hoerres

Artist's Profile

Monica Richards

Panorama City, California, USA

Monica Richards, best known for her musical side, "Faith and the Muse," is an internationally known artist, musician, and writer. She has released one full work, "The Book of Annwyn," which delves into the reworking of Welsh-Celtic tales, and is currently writing her second book, a treatise of poetic works from 1989 to the present. "In Lightning" is part of a larger piece, "Penelope."

In Lightning

It is the impossibility of womanhood that vexes me.
The femininity of reading eyes and minds—
The child bride symbol more fluid and sensual than desert waves,
The tiny bones of the wrist,
The organic movement to paint the lips—

I have eyes beneath seduction—
A face that beckons shadows—

And yesterday I wrote with the rhythm of lightning,
My page shocked to tiny platitudes of illumination,
Left breathless in the dark.

Words and sentences blindly scribbled
Crossing lines and scrawled meanings,
Metaphors stacked and snarled in brighter flashes.

Monica Vivienne Richards

All Your Names Are in Me

At dawn, your skin speaks to me through my skin like a drum-beat.
Tawny creatures of fur and feather, dance your dawn-names
In onion-skin colors across my sky.
And the ripples in water say your day-names
In endless knots of light and shadow.

At evening, your dusk-names echo in my chest
Like a savored breath of ocean air.
Pale sea creatures in colors of shell and tears
Swim-dance your dark-names in the corners of my eyes,
And all my steps feel a slippery pull
As though there is a tide that runs north to you.

All your names are in me.
Your names are in the fibers of my weave.
Your sun and moon are making a tapestry of me each day.
My threads seek you even across infinite,
Microcosmic gulfs of electrons and light,
Come to you even in the guise of common words,
Hinting at the song of you and me.

Nicholas I. Seigal

Cloudy Daze

Out in the world, I awake to the floating sound.
At the foot of my bed, the silver men orchestrate my thoughts
and dreams with a haunting image of little girls
with eyes in their teeth and arms on their feet.
My domesticated gray sleeps in the corner of the blue ceiling,
tied to a short leash, far away from the nose and ears of the non-believers.
Clouds outside bear down with black and white beards,
waiting for the next round of lightning and thunder to drip from the dark.
The wind in the air blows up in the trees
with all the birds and the shiny things.
Gazing through the window of sleep,
I watch the sun try to take a peek at what lives in the night.
I lie here all alone, feeling the cold breath of the ghost in my head
and listen to the hovering slowly fade.
The moon in my brain that reopened my mind
begins to wane into nothing.

Brian Briqueler

Artist's Profile

Laura Moisin

New York, New York, USA

James Joyce once proclaimed, "No man is an artist at all." E.E. Cummings wrote, "Kisses are a better fate than wisdom." Poetry is like a seizure, for whenever I think of the first line of a poem it is more the electrical impulse of a kiss than the wisdom inferred from generating an opus. But maybe Joyce is right, and I'm not an artist. Indeed, I'm content with being a good con artist convincing people, like my fervid fans (Michaela, Francesca, and Michael), that my thoughts are validated enough to appropriate into their lives.

Amenable

I live in a city of tall women and short men.
I live in a city and I'm somewhere in-between.
"I saw you last week," is what you said.
I saw you last week, and I hoped you'd say
on a savage, pilgrim frontier, on a crazy, milky jungle,
on a fantastic, upside-down ocean,
for it is there that I see myself.

I am created by my mind and my vision.
I am told to step lightly and look both ways.
My eyes cross and uncross, and my fingers uncross
against my forehead and my chest—two shoulders.
I see a line of solid poles surrounded by watchers,
and I am always moving and almost moved.
Dreary, I tell myself, but safe.
Depressing, I note, but stable.
Exciting, but impossible to let go.

I saw you the other day, and my heart almost drowned.
I saw you in myself and perhaps almost savagely restored.
Cross, uncross in the Sahara of my own, unintentional vastness.

Laura Moisin

Artist's Profile

Wang Jing

Central, South Carolina, USA

I am a Chinese teacher, and I love music and literature. To me, hope is cold as well as hot. Hope is the destination of achievements. It's always bigger than my life. To me, hope is not only a desire of living, but also a symbol of death. I have to use the power of poetry to break the limitations of time and space, to let my soul free at least. I live for it, and I will die for it, too!

Cold Like Hope

Cold like hope—
when my hope turned to white,
it was frozen into a fine statue,
molded on a boundless iceberg,
huge, heavy, but afloat.
A deer madly ran to chase the sun;
faster and faster like fire
raging across the land,
hungry and thirsty she ran,
straining ever faster
until her blood froze
and crashed on the land,
her body cold like hope,
her horns spread like fire.
The statue solidifies the last gesture of flying.

Wang Jing

Lithuanian Jewelry

Reserves of the Baltic,
translucent yellow, opaque black,
sit patiently in museum cases,
mold stubbornly to the carver's touch,
wait quietly in peddler's carts.

Succinum, spotted
with golden flecks, holds
ancient insects in its belly.

Jurate's tears, cries entrapped
by myth's whipping waves,
become baubles of
deep bronze hue.

Petrified resin,
thick, marmalade-colored stone,
finds itself near the clavicle
where bone greets bone.

Rebecca Bebe Leicht

Stepping from the Shower

She dries her hair with slow unstudied grace
and seeks her damp reflection through the steam;
a squeaky swipe on glass reveals a face
with features, finely drawn in peach and cream.

The towel drinks: A thirsty skill, displayed
in sips from neck and arms, from cleft and dune
of breasts, with nipples some capricious shade
of pink or beige according to the moon.

His scent precedes the creaking floorboard sounds;
she turns coquette, avoids his gaze and feigns
indifference: She sighs and tries on frowns
and yet, the shadow of a smile remains.

He claims her with a look and holds her still,
enjoying the appearance of the blush
suffusing on her cheeks against her will,
seducing without speaking—in no rush.

The people in the glass look back and stare:
Four pairs of eyes watch as he locks the door
and dims the light . . . she really doesn't care.
The towel lies forgotten on the floor.

Linda Taglio

Artist's Profile

Adi Dubash

Austin, Texas, USA

I'd like to think I've waited all my life to see my work in print. Now that it is, this is what I want the world to know: Dad, Mom, I owe my most prized possession—my mind—to your greatness as parents. Aunty Katy, this is more your success than mine. Jeena, you've always believed in me—thank you. To every reader, I pray for the individual in you.

Souzatska in the Rain

Like Souzatska in the rain,
I play a molar tune,
For you have gone.

Your footsteps on wet cobbles
Ripple grey memories
Of the music we had.

Each summer kiss,
A sugary note
Now drowned by florid waters.

Like Souzatska I stood
In the rain—
And leaky droplets
Touched smiling lips
As I wondered—of a world
Where tongues grow ripe
And old songs are never forgotten.

Adi Dubash

Waiting

In the old wooden rocker
at the top of the stairs
sits a doll long forgotten.
Dust decorates her hair.
Cobwebs trim the cotton of her dress.
She waits.

But the stairs have long been arduous
for the once little girl, now old.

So in the new cushioned rocker
at the bottom of the stairs
sits the weak little woman.
Memories decorate her eyes.
Forgotten conversations trim her mind.
She too waits.

Sylvia Biondich

Wrecked World

Your dishpan is quiet as a pond,
all the white ambition
shrunk to mild foam. You
have been away too long,
cups and plates tilt like glaciers.
Man, the toppler of worlds.
You wedge your hand
between what shifts
and slides, methodically
descend, layer by cool
layer, until your fingers crawl
along the smooth bottom—
amphibian.
This is where the knives lie,
mute battleships gone down
on their sides. How wonderful
to find them unaware
and then to pull one, nose up, and up
until it hangs in the stunned air—
wrecker in a wrecked world.

Sarfaraz Ahmed

Artist's Profile

Leah Kosmitis

Saint Petersburg, Florida, USA

I spun this poem at a time when I held much doubt and contempt for a certain person. I spent many hollow days and desolate nights pondering his possible feelings for me. This piece came about rather abruptly, and saved me from near insanity! Even now, my heart still jumps every time our eyes meet. I still cannot believe he is mine.

Entertaining an Element
of Boredom . . . One Night

If I could but touch the souls of so many.
He does not understand, for he turns away as I breathe.
Lies, I feel him as one escapes from a polluted rain.
It falls on my hands,
Drips off fingertips
Sore and cracked for trying too hard
Like dried petals of flowers,
Breaking where the sun is brutal.
And I escape from heat,
Relieved of your suppressing smile.
Words are not meant to sink a wall of irrevocable trust,
Covered by a silken touch of pure adoration.
If I sang, would you turn your shoulder?
Please! Can hurtful play cease
Under a plastic sky and warm moon?
Warm, yet hot, for this sky melts
With drips of waxy stars,
Falling on the lips of a cool, salty kiss
Echoing in the distance.
And I cry for empty promises.

Leah Michelle Kosmitis

Traffic

Day-after-day-after-day-after-day
That concrete heart pumps metallic cells
Through tarmac veins they flood and roll
In sinuous streams of white light glow
On cold flesh streets of silent conformity
Sinister crawling like blue smoke insects
Ants back to the nest with the green
That everyone chases restless blind
Bruised minds battered by routine hell trip
Numb unknown soul sad people of day
Eyes sting red strain behind glass prisons
Death row traffic lights at every turn
Restrict the flow with transient clot
That melts into heavy movement in time
Slow creep black rubber rolls in soft discs
Sometimes floats in Friday's short relief
As invisible chains lead back to the city
Chinking distant in claustrophobic night

Robert Graham Chisnall

Night before Winter

As the glowing sun slowly disappears
behind the white caps of the nearby mountains
marking the beginning of the upcoming winter,
I lie back in my chair,
sucked into the crackling, dried pages
of an old, delicate novel.
My mind continues to roam on,
as if I were traveling with the tale.
As time flashes past without me noticing,
the hooting of the owls
and the irritating squeaks of mice
finally pull me back to the present.
Naturally, my eyes go to the ticking clock above,
only to see that it is way past my sleeping hours.
It is then that I go rest,
resisting the temptation of another chapter.

Ota-Benga Ajayi Amaize

Artist's Profile

Lori Jerden

Slidell, Louisiana, USA

A few days after I wrote the poem, my ex asked me about the painting. I told him my friend's mother was sick and unable to paint the picture. I hated not telling the complete truth, but racism is a very real sickness in our society. People can and do change though. I got a message from the artist saying she had painted the picture! However, it would have to be purchased through an art dealer. More hedging on her part? If I were my ex and I knew the circumstances, I might not want the painting. Should I tell him about the artist afterall?

Magnolias in Taupe

He sat there gazing at the magnolia painting
Above my fireplace where it was hanging.
Asking of the artist, I was pleased to reply,
"She's the mother of a sweet friend of mine."
Admiring the piece, he continued to say
He'd love to commission the artist today.
Building a house, he had the perfect place.
"How soon?" he asked, excitement on his face.
His face is black, his smile is beautiful.
Our marriage is over, but love is mutual.
Practically one of the family despite my past.
She was eager to paint magnolias at last.
Wondering who the buyer might be,
She hedged and feigned for all to see.
My sweet young friend, embarrassed and sad,
The worst family fight they ever had.
"Never should've asked her," the father said.
Old South traditions are not dead.
I can't tell my ex, the truth is too ugly—
"The artist is sick," yes, she must be.

Lori Anne Jerden

Artist's Profile

Kristen Williams

Indiana, Pennsylvania, USA

Kristen Noel Williams earned a B.A. in English from Lycoming College (where she also obtained a minor in art history) and an M.A. in English from the University of Rochester. She is currently a teaching associate at Indiana University of Pennsylvania, where she is working towards a Ph.D. with a dissertation on mythological references in contemporary American women's poetry. This poem presents both the inner and outer selves we all contain and attempts to represent the struggle between the two in an artist's rendering so as to illustrate the all-too-frequent rift separating real sensibilities and their linguistic translations.

Chiaroscuro

like Janus, i have two faces:
one looking forward with hope,
the other, behind, with regret.
naturally, i am often trapped in the present
and neither fore nor aft looks
particularly appealing.

likewise, my colors are somewhat blessed
with contrast.
the lighter tones are merely a paler gray
fluted with silver, over which shadows
of black and scarlet swirl tumultuously.
i carry both palettes tirelessly, knowing
i am blank, undefined, without them.

but who would treasure the portrait as a
whole? porcelain skin and auburn eyes—
each necessary to enhance the other.
i can only wait, and hope not to fade
overmuch with the passing of time.

Kristen Williams

My Legacy

I am from where the red dirt meets the green jungle
The mangoes are plucked ripe off the trees
The juice runs clear down my chin
I am from the dark secrets carried in the bowels of slave ships
The rhythm of the Atlantic pushes us towards our destiny
I am from backs burnt from chopping cane
Ebony skin shines reflecting my beauty
I am from the place where palm trees whisper their stories
Nestled between their embraces my ears strain for their wisdom
Now, I am from the brownstones and basketball courts
Where baggy jeans and Timberlands are the standard uniform
I am from where bodegas are on every corner
Coronas are sipped, straw hats are worn, and dominoes are slammed
I am from a little seed that grew into an entire legacy

Morola Adjibodou

Dixie

Crack the coffee cup
and drip the heat between us.
Let it run over the table onto
this lap where you once sat.
What senseless irony, burn
the toast so you can't butter mine anymore.
Useless gestures, finding
crystal to spit your melon seeds
because a Dixie cup wasn't enough—
single black tears stuck in the carpet
these thirty years later,
caught in your web of lies,
still feeling the pricks in my feet
of the sorrys you spat at me.
Each one stuck deeper and deeper within.
Never accepting the paper-pink flowers
and baby blue, the witless humor of it all.
Thirty years and I can't hold our heat.

Keep your crystal; my coffee's cold.

Annie Lynn Oberg

E5

Completely smooth now,
Tuesday's activity migrates
Rapid red-eye with the wren,
Its echoes downsized.

The violator departs,
I'll lend an Oslo landing field
Late at night
Where the irony began.

The things we do to make you happy
Are all sold out,
Crowned a soul mate
Crowned a waste.

Lifeless is a kind of art,
A poet of the missing,
But I'm alert to the lack
And show it a new suffix.

Mark James Joesting

angel's wings

angel's wings drifting
down the face of your god
angel's wings dripping
with blood
by the hands of your god
unfair conviction
denied redemption
all is lost
souls are crossed
by this mighty, evil god
is it your choice
or is it his
where is your voice
are you wrapped up in sweet temptation
are you caught up in his molestation
he rapes your heart and steals your mind
banished from his kingdom
then to crawl back with no spine

April Jane Wheeler

Artist's Profile

Holly J. Helscher

Wyoming, Ohio, USA

Clarissa Pinkola Estes speaks of women who are "Angel Mothers." Julia is one of those individuals. Her consistent, gentle guidance and nurturing helped me turn a corner in my life at a time when I was confused and despairing. Since I have known her, she has helped me put a feminine face on the divine, and as a result, has helped me to see the feminine divine in myself. This poem is a tribute to her as a person and to the grace and wisdom she has bestowed upon me. The world is enriched because of her presence in it.

Julia

To she who has become my mother
You told me once that no one is more earthy than you.
Over time, I have come to understand what that means.

You wear yourself like a black panther,
elegant and graceful,
at home in the spaces you have chosen.

You speak your words like the evergreens,
poised and universal,
unwavering where they stand.

You share your spirit like the glistening moon,
gentle and consistent,
radiating light into shadow.

Connected to all that is,
your earthiness is like a spring meadow,
vibrant and welcoming to those who care to notice.

Holly J. Helscher

Artist's Profile

Larkyn Carpenter

Lincolnton, North Carolina, USA

My name is Larkyn O'Neill Carpenter, but one day I plan to use just Larkyn O'Neill as my stage name. I am 15 years old and hope to attend the N.C. School of Arts. I enjoy writing, acting, and drawing. My mother has been a big influence in my creative life. She is a writer and art lover. Our house is full of paintings and sculptures. I dedicate this poem to my best friend, Caren.

The Child

Strange, I believe I would throw up my hands
if you were the one to crucify me.
As I feel the fetus turn in me, the star shatters and
falls, not beautiful, but burning,
so that even my tears are heat.
Does she hear me? I try desperately to get through
the grabbing trees, to find her, but will I know her
now that she's taken the form of a small girl . . .
crying and crumpled in a heap on my bed.
The bedposts reach up high as if to kiss the clouds,
but instead they hit the ceiling.
I am standing outside the door, looking at your sleeping
body, watching the moon break through the fortress
of the curtains, to touch your fingertips.
I am witnessing you shrink from the starlight, and I'm
pounding my hands on the invisible barrier between us.
Oh, little girl, I feel you. Sometimes you become the
person crouched within me,
so hurt by the one who answered the invitation
to our thrown-up hands.

Larkyn Carpenter

Artist's Profile

Norisah Hashim

Wichita, Kansas, USA

This poem is a commiseration for the families of the victims of the tragedies of September 11, 2001, which touched and brought resentful tears of mixed feelings of anger, hate, and sympathy. Experiences of varied loss of loved ones show the feelings of regret within me. Was it the satanic human insanity or signs of quarterly flints of Doomsday? Only God the Almighty knows best.

The Last Supper

Yesterday
Disabled Mandy waited since crawling dawn
Till the moonless night breeze
Whispered between the unkept greys
Folded arms consoling the inclining stomach
Unfilled but a sip of sky juice
Dribble down an aging throat, winning the tears
Of hunger and longings for mashed potatoes and a glass of milk
Tales untold, messages undelivered
Retained an unanswered question
Stevie boy, why aren't you home yet?
Mama's cold and lonely
Beneath the trembled remains of the inclination towers
Slept in silence, but the streaming red
Stevie boy, breathless, lies, lips tight
Goodbye, Mama, I'll always love you

Norisah Hashim

On Seeing Yehuda Pen's Painting "Letter from America"

She looks like my grandmother: babushka wrapped,
Face stern with care not enmity,
Dark eyes hooded;
Protecting the last vestige of private dreams.

But it cannot be my grandmother.
The letter is from America,
The land of promises to which Grandma fled
So she would not have to wear her mother's face.

In her vagabond pack of rebellion,
Had Grandma mistakenly tucked her mother's face?
Had she taken from the old world age-old forbiddance
That thwarted dream-blossoming even in new soil?

Or was Grandma, like her mother, protecting a vision,
Distant but worthy of her patience,
That allowed her to glimpse herself
As the conduit to future care-free faces?

Sonya Oppenheimer

mourning music

sometimes felt like sugar-sweet morphine
slipped into my bloodstream
blood streamed
streaming flags
i could be you so
please no please no please no misguided retaliation
we all want blood and revenge
hell i'm thirsty too
but i could be you
i could be the ghostly
dust-covered man buried in the rubble
i could be
the innocent foreign-born man now in deep, deep trouble
so let's sing a song
honor the memory of naive and free america
because we're all grown ups now
we're all grown-up now
and dearest youthful america
i miss you already

Kent Brockman

Artist's Profile

Carolyn Comeaux

Rio Grande City, Texas, USA

For me, poetry is a way of preserving memories. Although I don't write many poems, I prefer writing novels, I use verse to remember the places and people I have loved and lost, and situations that over-whelmed me. In this poem, I speak of my two grandfathers. One, an old Cajun, house painter, and alcoholic, died young (at age 60), but quite suddenly; the other (at age 89), a retired salesman, died in a nursing home. As I grow older, my choice of death would be quickly on a sunny afternoon.

Two Grandfathers and a Prayer

Slumped over a sack of yellow feed corn,
he died in the afternoon
listening to squawks from hungry hens.
He lived wine days and whiskey nights;
his hands, rough as a splintered gate,
whispered when he touched me.
Drunk, his battered English cursed me.
Sober, his Cajun French teased me,
rippling like warm bayou water.

The other lives attached to doctors and pills;
a tube feeds through his nose.
His room smells of daffodils and feces;
he whispers of butchering days and catfish dinners in '36.
His hands idle, rest slack, yet he clings.

Sweet Jesus,
give me a swift life.
Curse me, tease me,
but touch me free
quickly
in the afternoon.

Carolyn Ann Comeaux

Another Language

It happens we must speak
another language
where waves beat against the rocks
like sheer white foam of consonants
Another language
than plain bread
and the rustling of money bills
Another language
than monotone intonations
of the anchorman's news reels
if not the almost unthinkable occurs
and invades his vain with stressing hormones

Another language
than the everyday semantics
and conversational reflections
Another language
where we can meet
in rare eye blinks
like star shots in the storm
and double rainbows
behind a red sun

Helge Johan Skigelstrand

Daddy

I didn't have to tell Daddy
that I hid under my covers
and talked to my teddy bears
when the dark made me scared
I didn't have to tell Daddy
that David and I found golf balls
in the front flower bed
when we were curious little kids
I didn't have to tell Daddy
when I didn't know what chicken pox were
the morning I woke up
with little, itchy spots on my skin
I didn't have to tell Daddy
that his words meant everything
his stories created my dreams
and his arms carried me through life
I didn't have to tell Daddy
because Daddy
always knew

Lauren Caudle

Artist's Profile

Donna Tuttle

Appleton, Wisconsin, USA

God gives eternal life to those whose lives have no sin. But not one person can ever meet this requirement. God knows this, and He loves you so much that He sent His Son, Jesus, to erase our sins forever. The funny thing is that God will not force eternal life upon you if you do not want it. You must first repent the things you know you've done wrong, and ask Jesus to forgive you for them. Jesus is faithful and true; He will forgive you when you ask Him to. Jesus will never leave you or forsake you. Friend, eternal life is yours, just ask for it!

Our Coffee Table

We built a coffee table, you and me.
Thirty plus years in construction, we built with care.
We made the foundation sure and strong. Nothing's wrong.
Forever molding it to our needs, it's respect.
We used it well: pumpkin pie, soda and life-changing stories.
The years go by fast, we etched in our marks
Of spots, stains, and scratches. Regardless, who sees a defect?

Why we threw that coffee table down the river that day, who can say?
The river had its way, the remains busted and broken.
Comfort ruined now, needs great repair.
Coziness gone, no longer fits us.
Awkward and useless, you thought we should hide it away.
Ever again, can it see the light of day?

How I miss our coffee table.
Nothing else around, nothing compares; our design was priceless.
Foundation, is it strong?
Repairs will be costly: time, commitment, and sacrifices.
Let's bring it out, you and me; we'll fix her.

Donna Tuttle

Artist's Profile

Marianne Miller

Tyler, Texas, USA

In 1976, soon after I moved to the Big Island of Hawaii ("Kona Side") to be near my children, I went sightseeing on the slopes of Mauna Loa ("Hilo Side"), and was stunned to come upon a single tiny yellow flower. It had thrust itself up through a hairline crack in a vast, black sea of hardened lava. In 1988, for my sixty-third birthday present (from me to me), I returned to America's mainland, the Big Island, to attend graduate school in Virginia. During a class in poetry writing, this poem about that precocious little flower was born.

Event on Mauna Loa

A fallen seed
from yesternight's bright flower
tumbles amid discarded husks
and humbled trees before
the crimson river's splayed
and crackling knees.
The red flood drags its dense
demented wake—seething,
heaving, blacktopping
root and reed.
Bedfellows strange beneath
the field—cinder and seed.
However deep the bed,
at some appointed hour,
with waft of dew and brush of light
fanning desire,
the seed commands its pavement dome.
It gives.
And, as all hope by hope is healed,
the flower lives.

Marianne "Jimi" Miller

The Garden

My son and I stand in his small backyard,
Discussing his vegetable garden.
The afternoon sun accentuates the fatigue in his face.
"These round holes in the lettuce leaves are harmless," he says,
Brushing aside a small, green worm.

Raking his fingers through the rich, moist soil,
He exposes several sow bugs and speaks quietly about
The cycle of life and the value of all living things.
Even the insects.
No need to shorten their life span with pesticides.

We move through the narrow side-yard gate
Where he proudly shows me his snow peas
Stretched by strings up the side of the fireplace.
He fills my hands with peas and I promise
That they will be eaten tonight.

My son's wife waves to us from the kitchen window.
She smiles.
She is young, thin, and beautiful.
She is wearing her new wig.
She has cancer.

Pat Beck

Sunday Dinner

There is no Sunday dinner.
Once there was.
Crisp linen was spread on the wood table.
Mother would cook for anyone
coming through that old front door.
While soup simmered, Grandmother complained.

A bag of dirty laundry
brought by a young married couple
wound up in the washing machine.
Clean sheets flapped on the line.
Uncle scrutinized by the women rolling pie dough
wondering why he never took a wife
like he was expected to.

There is no one to drop in on now.
Strangers live in that house
with locks that have no keys for us.
We can run to friends for temporary
comfort without history.
But there is no Sunday dinner.
Once there was.

Janice L. Jakubowitcz

Artist's Profile

Micayla Naomi Nelson

Saint Charles, Missouri, USA

I dedicate my achievement to my friends and family. Thank you to my mother for being my angel for the past sixteen years. Thank you, Mr. Meier, for being an excellent mentor and friend, and teaching me to put my thoughts onto paper. Thank you, Meagan, for being the best friend any girl could hope for. And thank you, Chris, for inspiring me in every aspect, and making me the luckiest girl in the world. I love you the most, baby.

Kingdom

It was just us in our kingdom—
a simple courtyard of cool green grass
encircled by cream colored concrete that was
toasted warm in the afternoon sun
and chilled in the pale indigo evenings.
In our kingdom,
we were superheroes with beach towel-
capes and pine cone grenades . . .
we were princesses with clover crowns
and 25¢ lip gloss . . .
Sometimes, we would sit barefoot in the dewy
summer grass and watch, with popsicles bleeding
their sugary nectar over our scraped
knuckles, as shades of evening rolled over
the oranges, yellows, and purples of a fading
sunset.
We were all alone then;
Just me and my friends, all alone, in our own
kingdom.

Micayla Naomi Nelson

Artist's Profile

Daniel Peter Juda

New York, New York, USA

Asked for decades to return to Germany, my father said "No." But when he reached his eighties, this descendent of the Kempinski (Hamburg) Clan, whose life (and mine) had been forever altered by the Third Reich, said "Yes." I have never seen him happier (he re-met his best high school pal) or sadder as he revisited his youth (of bliss and terror). I commemorate this poem to our one-week visit to Berlin together with 200 Jewish survivors, guests of the German government.

Return to Berlin

We returned
mein Herr
marching over
buried memories

We returned
Walter
but you dared not enter YOUR home
now a Gestalt Therapy Clinic

We returned dad
and even the head-splitting ambivalence
did not halt the laughter in your step

We returned
with 200 aged invited survivors
but the copper plaque on the Kempinski wall
did not salve the family wound

We returned the few remaining
traumatized and triumphant
trodding atop Hitler's tomb.

Daniel Peter Juda

Vivid Abstraction

Everything is as it was
Or as it might have been
If it hadn't been for you
Being for me when we were

Light showing dust where it is
Where it used to be
When it wasn't visible
In that same old spot

I have found the underneath
Up above where it shouldn't be
Where it has always been
Though it should never have made it this far

I've packed it away in boxes, in frames
Though it's boundless
Which makes it more appealing when contained
Easier to focus upon

So much more visible now that it's lost
Found through abandonment
Multiplying when broken at last
Lighter now but better at weighing me down

Erin Elizabeth Spatz

Don: Nouveau Hippie

Overalls held together only by the paste
Of his sweat and grime
Cut off mid-thigh
Dingy threads dangle to his knees
Ribs raising the red
Of his cotton T-shirt
Pit stains peek
Seeping from under skinny arms
Shiny, silver cell phone
Clipped to his pocket
Receiver of a pay phone
To his ear
Nest of nappy gray hair
From the top of his head
To the bib of his overalls
Hiding his smile
Except in his eyes

Kathleen Gayle Perry

Artist's Profile

Devdatta Das

Pune, India

I come from an obscurity called Tezpur, the ancient "City of Eternal Love"—the imperial child of the river Brahmaputra. And I am the sunshine from there, where ripples are still called waves. My verses are attempts to search for spaces where the divisions of father/child, day/night, master/slave, man/woman, and succumbing/fortitude blur into a luminous cognizance. Where hope is eternal and reality is ephemeral, my verses, tributes to my father and mom, are driven by the darmon who sits on the rock of Mt. Olympus with a foot in the waters of the Red River, the Brahmaputra.

Oscillations

I sat beside the window, naked,
A bulge half shadowed the light,
Pregnant thoughts at pregnant times.
Had I been him,
I would've made love and
Still been in shape nine months later.
If only God made me man!
Laborious pains (?) and pregnant thoughts;
I burnt my lungs in the lobby
Waiting for the first wail to emanate from eternity.
Ah!
I held her close to my breasts,
The little head and still
Blue cord dangling at the navel.
I rushed inside—into the room.
Ah!
What a sight to see—
My only, my daughter.
Blurred thoughts and the genes intervene
Every time,
Oscillating, oscillating, oscil . . .

Devdatta Das

Pieces

I saw another:
a flower in a field of weeds,
an island in a sick tormented sea
of parasites and marauders,
holding fast to what is now known
and what is familiar.

The wind has touched her before,
but she would no longer succumb to its will.
She must be what she must be,
else be lost to the sea at sea
and never see another day.

O. Rashaan Austin

Joint Meeting

You sit on the other side of the table.
For those around us, we are strangers,
you greeted me, "Madame,"
I called you by your title, "Excellence."
But elsewhere, I call you, "my love,"
and you hold me into your arms.
You look haughty, but I know your smile,
your face when you love me.
I know the way you sleep, how you wake up.
Obviously, you are getting bored.
You cross and uncross your hands,
your wonderful hands so smooth
when you touch me.
You do your job. I do mine.
But above all, I have in front of me
two blessed hours to stare at you, my love,
secretly, nobody noticing, even you.
I love joint meetings, where you are there,
on the other side of the table.

Daniele Delcourt

Artist's Profile

Mark Haggarty

San Francisco, California, USA

A poem is time by yourself, to your thoughts. After love in the morning and while she sleeps again, you watch the dawn. A poem is drifting off to sleep and finding that perfect spot where your body feels truly eased. A poem is awakening like a bolt in the middle of the night, fumbling for the light, and furiously writing out a poem before the idea leaves you. I love baseball, but never hit well enough. I love music, but couldn't play instruments. But I could always write, and so here we are.

Simply

Can you and I always be touching?
I mean even times when we're
Buried in the couch and
Reading separate books, totally engrossed.
Can we remain yet in contact
Somehow, like our legs slowly rubbing
Up against one another's
And our toes can be touching?

And when we sit and smile someday
In green vinyl lawn chairs
At the beach, wearing UV-blocking sunglasses,
Deaf to the monotonous ocean crashing,
Our hands, you know, might start digging
Through the sand and tunnel together,
One last give and we'll break through.
We could be touching, then
Keep your hand there, okay?

No thought makes me happier
Than sandy fingers clasping in the cool damp.

Mark Francis Haggarty

After You Died

You know what I did after you died?
I rounded up all your straws,
the ones you used to reach all the way to the bottom
of the Absolut bottle.
That was after you stopped using glasses, ice cubes, and mixes.

I filled all the straws with cement,
and when they were hard I sharpened each one to a spear-like point.
I implanted them in the dirt above you,
one 1/2 inch from the other.
When I was done, and your grave blanketed
by a multitude of tiny obelisks pointing to the sky,
I lay upon them, and
I sobbed and sobbed.

Len McCawley

Existential

You are my Apollo.
You laugh and dance in darkness; I stumble over your imprints.
Your teasing eyes seduce me to follow
and, all too willingly, I go where you go,
pretending to play your sidekick; pretending to be your co-star.
Apollo, do not walk so fast.
Do not disappear from the presence of this abyss.
Your cynical hands caress my tears before they have a chance to fall.
Dare I dance your evil, cosmic legacy to life?
Dare I beg your planets to pass on by?
I dare not. For I am through pretending.
You are not Apollo nor am I your star.
Millions of years have long been gone
since we looked into the cratered stares of one another.
Dare I recall? Dare I forget? We are not contained by one universe.
We are separate galaxies, Apollo, we are not one.
Shall we wait another million years to orbit each other once more?
Or shall we chance it to infinity?
The black sun rises and there are no moons. No stars. No planets.
Have there ever been?

Roxanne Hack

Artist's Profile

Josette Fernandes

New Bedford, Massachusetts, USA

I have been writing since I was about five years old. For me, writing is as necessary as air and sleep. "Temper the Violets" is a reflection of the nameless force that has compelled me to put pen to paper for so long. It's a poem of dreams, wishes, and the strength we sometimes need to see ourselves through the more difficult times in our lives. I am truly honored that I have been given a chance to share this poem with others.

Temper the Violets

Temper the violets,
Do not let them grow wild.
The primordial soup of pre-Christian times,
Sweet Jesus! Have I known Thee?
Lest we forget we are but modern men,
Alone in the times of our well-being.
Lessen not the rope which is fastened about my neck.
Knotted splendor,
I beseech thee.
Temper not the violets,
But save one for me.

Josette Fernandes